THE MAGIC OF A TIDY HOME

The Proven Method for Turning Your Home into a Place of Peace, Joy and Productive Life

By Joy Ferguson

THE MAGIC OF A TIDY HOME

Contents

FOREWORD 1
INTRODUCTION 3
ABOUT THE AUTHOR 7
DEDICATION 11
ACKNOWLEDGEMENTS 13
CHAPTER 1
THE POWER OF HABIT 15
CHAPTER 2
THE KITCHEN 29
CHAPTER 3
THE BATHROOM 45
CHAPTER 4
THE LIVING AREA 55
CHAPTER 5
THE RUMPUS/FAMILY ROOM 65
CHAPTER 6
THE BEDROOMS 75
CHAPTER 7
THE WORKING AREAS 95
CHAPTER 8
THE GARAGE AND GARDEN SHED 111
CONCLUSION 123

THE MAGIC OF A TIDY HOME

FOREWORD

"It's no secret that clutter can affect our stress levels, our ability to focus and our sleep. This explains why the quote "a cluttered space is a cluttered mind" has been endorsed by so many people.
So, if you too are determined to be more organised and get on board the decluttering craze, this is the book for you. Joy's methods for tidying up and organising space are easy and very effective. Joy will help you transform your space and find peace of mind all while having fun!"

Pat Mesiti

Best selling author and international speaker

THE MAGIC OF A TIDY HOME

INTRODUCTION

Have you ever wondered why it can be so difficult to have a tidy home? Do you feel that you don't have enough storage space? Do you know what you have in your storage spaces? Do you have anything you haven't used for at least 12 months? Do you keep things because there is bound to be a "just in case" moment in your life where you might be able to use it? Can you imagine living in a tidy home, with ample storage space for everything, and be so organised that you can immediately locate anything you need?

I have seen people go so far as to extend the size of their home in order to have extra space for everything. The extra space is soon filled and "hey presto" things are back to how they were prior to extending their home. I know people who have tried to down-size or declutter and have no idea where to start. I have seen toy boxes overflowing with toys. There are refrigerators and pantries overflowing with food, vanity cupboards at more than capacity with product, and wardrobes so full the doors won't close.

I spent my childhood in a tidy environment, however, many years later after becoming a mother, I found it necessary to explore new ways of keeping a tidy home. I am excited to share with you what I did to stay on top of everything during those wonderful years when my children were living at home.

Another challenge presented itself when my beloved widowed mother passed away and the contents of her home ended up in mine. I found it was not possible to fit the contents of two houses into one. Hence, I began a huge decluttering exercise, made more difficult by the fact that there were many of my mother's belongings which had sentimental value to me.

In recent years I have relocated a number of times. Sure, I managed to get rid of some of my "stuff", however, there were still dozens of boxes to pack each time I moved. I couldn't bring myself to part with my things. I now understand why my dear mother had the best intentions when she would say she was going to get rid of everything she had packed away that was no longer of any use to her. I also understand why she found it difficult to make a start on sorting through everything.

I know that many people out there can relate to how my mother and I felt when we thought about decluttering. My mother's home was always tidy, and I wouldn't have thought she had so many things to dispose of. However, I discovered differently following her passing. Similarly, my home appeared tidy. Then I discovered that this was because I was an expert at storing things in cupboards. The problem with having cupboards packed with all those things is when it comes time to find something, the whole cupboard has to be dismantled to locate the item. Then everything has to be packed away again. Sometimes it becomes easier to go out and purchase a new item, rather than look for the one you know you have stored away somewhere. Then a place needs to be found to store the new item. We all know what is happening here. Quite a vicious cycle is being established, isn't it?

How many people identify with what I have described? Do you know what you possess and where you have stored it? Is it easy to locate when you need it? Can you find that lid for the container which you just put the potato salad into? Can you find that lipstick which matches your outfit? You know you have the perfect

INTRODUCTION

colour somewhere. What happened to that school sock? The bus is coming down the road and the sock is nowhere to be found. Where is the oven mitt? The casserole is cooked and needs to be removed from the oven. The meal is ready to be served. Has the cutlery been washed or is it still in the dishwasher or sink? The weather has changed and, instead of warm clothing, you need something cooler to wear. You have gained a little weight over the cooler months and are not sure what clothes in your wardrobe still fit. You have to be at an appointment in a short time. How will you feel when everyday living becomes hassle-free? Just like magic, you will have a tidy home. You will always be able to find things. You won't have to waste time searching through overflowing cupboards, pantries and refrigerators. It will be so much easier to keep up with the washing, vacuum the floors, and get out the door on time for appointments.

I have written this book to share how to make magic happen for you. I know that you can have an organised life and a tidy home, and that is why I am excited about walking with you step by step through every room and cupboard in your home to make this happen for you.

Please turn the page, read my story, and we will get started in Chapter 1 to discover how magic can happen for you too.

THE MAGIC OF A TIDY HOME

ABOUT THE AUTHOR

I grew up on a dairy farm in the foothills of the Bunya Mountains which are approximately 160kms north west of Brisbane, Queensland, Australia. I am the eldest of three children, my younger siblings are brothers. I count my blessings every day that my parents were people who loved to be organised. My mother always had a tidy home. She had developed a routine which she followed each day. My father displayed similar qualities with his farm buildings and machinery sheds. He even had an orderly way of keeping his farm records of income and expenditure for the tax man.

There is a beautiful poem written by Dorothy Law Nolte, Ph.D. titled "Children Learn What They Live". There is a line in that poem which says, "If children live with praise, they learn appreciation". I remember my mother walking into our house which I had cleaned and tidied while she was milking the cows. With a look of appreciation on her face, she praised me for doing the housework and conveyed to me how much it meant to her. I believe that is where I learnt appreciation for having a clean and tidy house. My bedroom was always tidy. My dolls were never left lying around. In fact, they were my babies and I tucked them into their cots and put their clothes away after I finished playing with them. I always knew where I could find everything. My mother never found it necessary to remind me to tidy up my room. I simply followed what I had learned from her.

During my time at high school in Kingaroy, rough, dirt roads made it necessary for me to board in town from Monday to Friday. My habits of being tidy and organised were appreciated by the people with whom I lived until I married. While I was engaged in employment as a bookkeeper, my desk was always tidy. Because I spent many years living out of a suitcase, I developed a style of packing which enabled me to easily locate what I needed for each day. My husband and I lived in Kingaroy where we were blessed with our beloved family of six children. My organisational efforts were challenged somewhat while rearing our family. However, it was a much-cherished opportunity for me to develop some new approaches to being as organised as possible while, at the same time, juggling my role as a mother.

We began a farming venture which entailed moving with our six children to an area near Hervey Bay. We set up house in a large shed on our farm for a few years before renting a house in the Bay, then building our beautiful six-bedroom home in the next street.

ABOUT THE AUTHOR

After a few years, I moved to Brisbane and the children attended primary and secondary schools at McGregor and tertiary education at Griffith University at Nathan.

Now that my children have grown up and left home, I find myself with time to pursue other interests. I receive a great deal of enjoyment from reading house and garden magazines. My bookshelf contains many books about gardening, cooking, health and personal development.

My new phase in life includes the pleasure of being a grandmother many times over. While the grandchildren were young, I appreciated their parents insisting that the children put their toys and books into the designated storage places in readiness for their next visit. This helped me to get my house back to a tidy state, and I trust the children learnt what being tidy could do for them.

I have moved and set up house many times throughout my life and have learnt many organisation skills during these moves. I have now moved to a two-bedroom unit and have added the skills of down-sizing which comes with another set of challenges.

I am grateful for the living experiences I have gained throughout my life beginning with living out of a suitcase for six years to moving from units to a shed to houses of varying sizes and now to completing the down-sizing venture. I am now using my experience to help readers create organised, tidy homes to align with their life circumstances.

THE MAGIC OF A TIDY HOME

DEDICATION

I dedicate this book to my family. Thanks to Mum and Dad for being an example to me in being tidy. Thanks to my children and grandchildren for strengthening my ability to be tidy in the midst of what sometimes could have been chaos. I love you all.

THE MAGIC OF A TIDY HOME

ACKNOWLEDGEMENTS

Thank you to Pat and his many speakers I have been privileged to meet and learn from. Thank you to my friends for believing in me when I didn't believe in myself. Thank you to Donna-Marie for guiding me through many steps on my journey. Thank you to Laura for valuable lessons in maintaining emotional balance. Thank you to Corinna and her team for editing and producing my book. Thank you to Steven and Darren for giving me kicks in the pants along the way.

THE MAGIC OF A TIDY HOME

CHAPTER 1

THE POWER OF HABIT

Many people have jumped into a massive clean-up of their homes, tidying everything and putting everything away into cupboards, and experiencing how great it feels to have every nook and cranny clean and tidy. They walk around taking a look at how great it all appears, experience the feeling of being organised, and vow and declare that this is how things are going to be from here onwards. Then a week or two later it has returned to how it was prior to the tidy-up. They might be thinking what a waste of time and effort that huge exercise was. The main reason this happens is because it was a short-term event in the form of a quick fix, and there was no follow up on how to maintain it. Mindset, habits and rules need to be established in order to maintain a tidy state.

What is a mindset?
A mindset is the established set of attitudes held by someone.

Why is mindset so important?
Having a growth mindset (the belief that you are in control of your own ability, and you can learn and improve) is the key to success. Yes, hard work, effort, and persistence are all important, but not as important as having that underlying belief that you are in control of your own destiny.

How is mindset formed?
Your mindset is rooted in your experiences, education, and culture from which you form thoughts that establish

beliefs and attitudes. Those thoughts, beliefs, and attitudes lead to certain actions and with those actions you have experiences. Those experiences give your mind new information to process.

How can I have a cleaning and organising mindset?
You may feel you don't have the time or energy to always have a tidy home, and you have fallen into a scarcity mindset of 'What's the use, it doesn't stay tidy for long?" "I probably don't deserve to have a clean, organised home." "I am too tired after being at work all day." However, you remember how great you felt after you had cleaned and tidied up. You also know it took effort to get it that way and that you were the one who made it happen.

Mindset can be changed by changing your thoughts. You may be feeling that household chores are a drag and something that has to be done whether you feel like doing it or not.

When changing to a mindset of self-care, "I am doing this for me, so that I can feel great when I walk into a clean and tidy home after work," and, "I deserve to feel proud of my clean and tidy home when visitors come to see me," you will be amazed how much energy you have. If you have children, you are setting an example for them to learn from.

What is a habit?
A habit is a settled or regular tendency or practice, especially one that is hard to give up.

How long does it take to form a habit?
There are varying thoughts on this subject. The most common belief held is 21 days. The 21/90 rule is about

building a habit and making it a permanent lifestyle change. It takes 21 days to build a habit and 90 days to make it a permanent lifestyle change. Commit to your goal for 21 days and it will become a habit. Commit to your goal for 90 days and it will become a part of your lifestyle. Small children for example, love to please their parents. It is much easier to teach them as they are learning to do things for themselves than having to correct them further down the track. As they are learning to dress themselves, teach them how to keep their clothing tidy in their drawers. When they undress, teach them where to put their dirty clothes. Before they handle food, remind them to wash their hands with soap and water. These actions will become habits, and, before long, there will be no need for reminders.

There is an area of the brain called the "basal ganglia" and this is where habits are found. The more often an action is performed or the more often behaviour is repeated, the more it becomes physically wired into the brain. This stimulates a specific neuronal pattern and becomes strengthened in the brain. This can work either way. Tidy habits are going to make everyday living easier and the opposite is going to cause chaos.

End clutter by having places for everything and putting everything back into place after use. This simple act makes tidiness easier to achieve and maintain. For example, place dirty clothes into the laundry hamper, fold clean clothes and place them into the cupboard, take children's unused or outgrown clothes to the charity shop or pass them down to a younger child, use worn-out tea shirts for cleaning rags, and store them in a 'rag bag', which can be made from a piece of material or a pillowcase. It is best not to use plastic bags as most are recyclable these days, and they create a mess in the cupboard when they begin to break down.

Life works better for everyone when there are rules to follow.

What is a rule?
A rule is one of a set of explicit or understood regulations or principles governing conduct or procedure within a particular area of activity.

Notice when a child starts school there are rules to be followed every day. They learn where to place their lunchboxes and drinks, their books, and where to store their school bags and hats. If they catch a bus to school, there are rules to follow to keep them safe. If they ride a bike, there are rules for keeping them and other children safe, and places at school where their bikes are stored each day. If they walk to school, there are rules about walking on footpaths and using pedestrian crossings. The lollypop people do an amazing job in keeping children safe when crossing the road and they too follow rules. When children realise that parents, teachers and lollypop people have their best interests at heart, they will more readily accept that rules are best followed, and this allows for safety and happiness for all. Imagine how chaotic a classroom or playground would be if there were no rules.

The same principles can work at home. When rules or boundaries are set and followed, everything runs smoothly because everyone knows what is expected. Engage all family members in deciding which is the best way for everything to run and how it affects each member of the family. Children are more likely to enjoy having rules if they are part of making them and can see the benefits for themselves and each person involved.

Rules have the dual purpose of setting children up for life when they are living independently.

Less is best when it comes to the number of rules required. Two or three rules keep everything simple and are easily remembered. Much is written on the internet and in magazines about this topic and many good books have been written too.

The following rules are an example and can easily be learnt by every family member, including children as young as 4:
Rule 1: We are kind and respectful to ourselves.
Rule 2: We are kind and respectful to others.
Rule 3: Families help each other.

Rule 1: Being kind and respectful to ourselves could mean making our beds and keeping our bedrooms tidy, not beating ourselves up if we fail a school test or lose a game, taking care of our personal hygiene.
Rule 2: Being kind and respectful to others could mean using our manners, listening carefully to what someone is saying to us, showing kindness when someone is hurt, being happy for others' successes, covering our mouths when coughing or sneezing, washing our hands before meals, not being loud and noisy inside the home.
Rule 3: Families help each other could mean putting our plates and cutlery in the sink after a meal, hanging our towels after showering, placing our dirty clothes into the laundry hamper, carrying the shopping from the car to the kitchen, being ready to leave for school on time to avoid the stress of being late, getting our homework done at the appropriate time, getting to bed at the designated time each night.

THE MAGIC OF A TIDY HOME

A fun thing to do for younger children to feel part of the plan is to take an A4 sheet of paper and write or type the 3 family rules on it, leaving space at the bottom for a drawing. Make one for each child's bedroom and one for the refrigerator as a reminder of the rules. Have each child decorate his/her paper with their name and a drawing. Place each completed sheet into an inexpensive photo frame, then stand it or hang it in a place in their respective bedrooms where it can easily be seen, to serve as a reminder, while at the same time serving as décor for each room.

At first, benefits of rules may not be appreciated, however, in time with persistence and consistency, family members will come to appreciate how much their lives improve when everyone is following the rules. Children will see how much they benefit when they follow the household rules, especially when they get to do what they love and appreciate. They will be encouraged as they observe their parents sticking to the rules. They will feel valued as a family member when everyone is working together for the good of the whole household. Children have been known to check each other at times. For example, one child might be breaking a rule by using a profanity and a sibling will point out that 'our family doesn't use that word', and so on. It is worth remembering that without reinforcement, rules can easily fall by the wayside and everything returns to chaos and disorder.

Workplaces have rules for smooth operation too. The procedures manual is worth its weight in gold, especially in offices or fast-food outlets. McDonalds staff, for instance, have a set way of serving customers and preparing orders. Other franchises have similar sets of guidelines, thus making duplication simple. The manual is a document that provides instructions or guidelines on how to perform an activity and serves as a reference book on the activity. Rules for work commencement and finishing times and lunch breaks are further examples. When a new staff member joins the organisation, remembering what to do and how to do it is set out in the manual, ensuring that nothing is forgotten or completed incorrectly.

There are rules for every area of life. When traffic rules are followed, it is safer for us to drive on our roads. Examples are obeying traffic lights, road signs and speed limit signs, using seat belts correctly, driving on the correct side of the road, negotiating intersections safely, using turning indicators, breaking safely, avoiding the use of mobile phones while driving, and safely carrying children in vehicles.

The place in which we live and the way in which we live have an effect on every part of our lives. Imagine a scenario where everything is in disarray in the home. It is morning and the parents have to get to work on time and the children have to get to school before the first bell, so there are deadlines to meet. There are dishes in the sink from the night before, the dirty clothes are strewn all over the floors in various rooms, there are wet towels thrown on the floor in the bathroom. Homework hasn't been completed and is due to be handed in that day. There is no milk in the refrigerator for breakfast and no bread for school lunches. This is certainly not a great start to a happy, successful day.

Now, imagine the same scenario, only this time a few minutes have been spent the night before, in preparation for the next morning. The dishes have been placed in the dishwasher and the dishwasher has been switched on, or they have been washed and stacked in the dish drainer. The dirty clothes have been placed in the laundry hamper and the towels have been hung in the bathroom. The milk and bread have been taken care of during the recent shopping trip, or they have been picked up by one of the parents on the way home from work the previous day. The homework has been completed before the evening meal. All it takes is a small amount of forward planning which becomes a habit. Having lists can be a useful tool for ensuring that nothing is forgotten.

Being tidy and organised and having a daily routine are qualities that give back a hundred-fold over time. It all begins with small steps, and, when it becomes a daily habit, saves the family members time and prevents frustration. There is nothing to argue about, no blaming for things going wrong and no stressful last-minute situations. Best of all, everyone benefits from extra time to do fun things when the weekends roll around. All of this happens daily when thought is applied. For example, when clothes are removed, it doesn't take any more time to place them in the laundry hamper than the time it takes to throw them on the floor. Hanging the towels takes a minute at most. When taking off shoes, rather than leaving them in the middle of the floor where someone can easily fall over them, simply place them where they are meant to be stored and they will never become lost. Place the socks in the laundry hamper.

It sounds easy to establish rules, however the tricky part is following them. Rules are a waste of time if there is no follow through. Persistence is the key however, if something doesn't work as well as first thought, then change it. Every household operates differently, therefore it can take time to come up with something that works well for each particular household. Modifying or altering rules is not a sign of failure. It is merely the act of finding what works best. Start by making a list of everything that needs to be done. Include time for taking care of health and sleep. Being together as a family to eat dinner at night in a relaxing manner benefits the digestive system, lessens anxiety and strengthens family relationships. Getting to bed at a reasonable time promotes good sleep that is vital to providing enough energy to be able to function the next day. We all want the best for our families and the best doesn't happen without effort.

Why is the family meal important?
For many busy parents, it would be much easier and simpler to forget about family dinners. Jobs, children, after-school activities all contribute to families being constantly on the go, thus feeling the need to eat on the run. However, many parents are realising the importance of shared family time at the dinner table, particularly when distractions such as the television are turned off. This is often the only time when all family members are together in one place.

Family dinners can be viewed as another job to do at the end of a day, or a time for family members to share the day's events with each other. Common topics include school and sports, friends and social events, and even minor family issues and problems. It is best to deal with major issues and problems at another time in order to avoid upsetting or confronting situations during meals. Family mealtime needs to be an enjoyable, happy experience in order to give family members the opportunity to relax and unwind after a busy day. It helps them to handle the stresses and hassles of day-to-day existence.

THE MAGIC OF A TIDY HOME

Eating together tends to promote more sensible eating habits. Good table manners can be taught, as well as listening to one another, learning how to listen, and learning to respect one another. Dinner time is a perfect opportunity to build self-esteem in children. By listening to what they have to say, you are saying, "I value what you do; I respect who you are and what you're doing; what you do is important to me." Mealtime can be viewed as an opportunity or as a chore. If it's viewed as an opportunity, then all sorts of possibilities are created; if it's viewed as a chore, then the possibilities don't exist. Having a regular family dinner time can enhance family dynamics. Children who feel valued are more likely to connect with the family goal of having a tidy home.

Tidying your home and keeping it that way on a daily basis has many benefits over tidying weekly, monthly or yearly. Some of us are morning people while some of us are evening people. Morning people love to get out of bed early and get things done each morning. Evening people prefer to sleep into the morning and go to bed later at night. This presents challenges for people who have to be at work early or who have children who have to arrive at school before the first bell. Alarm clocks aren't the ideal way to wake up each morning, however, sometimes it is necessary until a habit is formed. It is important to leave enough time to complete everything necessary before leaving home each morning. Remember to leave a few minutes to make your bed each day.

Making your bed means much more than 'just another job to be done'. It can set you up for the whole day, and, in fact, a whole lifetime. The defence force places huge importance on this simple act. In his Commencement Address in 1914, at the University of Texas at Austin, Admiral William H McRaven, Commander, United

States Special Operations Command, delivered a wonderful speech to 8,000 graduates. He stated that, in his rigorous training as a navy seal, the first task of the day was to make his bed to perfection. He stated that, "if you make your bed each morning you will have accomplished the first task of the day. It will give you a small sense of pride. It will encourage you to do another task and another and another, and by the end of the day that one task completed will have turned into many tasks completed. Making your bed will also reinforce the fact that little things in life matter. If you can't do the little things right, you'll never be able to do the big things right. If by chance you have a miserable day, you'll come home to a bed that is made, a bed that you made. A made bed gives you encouragement that tomorrow will be better". There have been best-selling books written about the act of making your bed. Need I say any more about how important it is to make your bed?

At first you could be forgiven for thinking it is all too difficult and time consuming. You might be thinking 'when am I going to have time to do everything else?' and 'I don't want to be doing housework all day'. You will soon discover that, when the habits are formed, you will have everything under control and be able to experience the magic of a tidy home.

Our homes are where everything in life stems from. Homes tell us a lot about the people who live there. Our physical and mental wellbeing depends to a major extent on our living environment. If someone is experiencing difficulty in coping emotionally in certain areas of life, their home can easily fall into disarray. This can have a crippling effect on mental wellbeing. Firstly, the sufferer is unable to find the motivation to tidy up, and secondly, the untidier the home becomes, the further down the spiral the sufferer falls. People with temporary or permanent physical disabilities also experience challenges. In fact, when homes are altered to allow for wheelchairs, walking frames or crutches, people are able to live independently either alone or in a family.

From toddlers to elderly folk, independence is something which everyone strives for. Toddlers have no concept of safety and they will always find a way to climb to where they want to be. A safe stepping stool will assist them greatly in reaching the handbasin tap for handwashing. Access ramps and wider doorways and hallways make life much easier for those in wheelchairs. Non-slip floor rugs or no rugs at all and grab-rails in showers and toilets help to prevent accidents for people using crutches and walking frames.

When people feel safe and in control of their circumstances at home, they are more likely to experience happiness and wellbeing, which can influence their whole day ahead.

A tidy home doesn't have to be absolutely spotless at all times, with no single item out of place, leaving no time for doing other things. When reading an issue of "Time Life" magazine recently, I came across a quote which read, "Time is a finite resource, and sometimes it is better spent on a tickle fight than scrubbing the bathroom clean", and I agree wholeheartedly with this. Having a tidy home is about balancing what really matters with what is being unnecessarily fastidious, especially while children are still living at home. That being said, however, children learn by example. If they live in a tidy environment, they learn to appreciate tidiness, and they discover that losing things doesn't occur nearly as often. This, in turn, saves time and minimises frustration.

I will tell you a story from my own life when my six children were young and all still living at home. When I would set up the sewing machine with the intention of making clothes for my family, my children would bring out all their teddy bears for me to sew clothes for. After a few hours, we had very excited children, a messy house, well-dressed teddy bears and no new clothes for the family. However, we had enjoyed so much fun and laughter together, that it didn't matter. I found time on another day to do what I set out to do, and it really didn't take much time to put the house back in order. The happy looks on my children's faces far outweighed the importance of a tidy home and created beautiful memories for us all. It reminded me that there is never a mess that couldn't be cleaned up.

We can be very grateful for the fact that we have a home to live in. There are many people out there who don't share this privilege. With this in mind, let's now work through one room at a time and get the magic of a tidy home happening for you.

THE MAGIC OF A TIDY HOME

CHAPTER 2

THE KITCHEN

The kitchen is the heart of the home. It is the place where beautiful childhood memories are made. There is something sacred about food and, without it, we would not survive. Many wonderful and meaningful conversations take place in the kitchen. Having plenty of natural light streaming in has the potential to lift the mood of the people engaged in kitchen activities.

One of my dearest memories goes back to when my beloved late mother regularly came to spend a week or two with us. We would enjoy a meal together, and what happens after a meal? Of course, the dishes have to be washed. We didn't have a dishwasher in those days, so my Mum, my two daughters and I would gather around the kitchen sink. We would have so much fun chatting and laughing, sometimes hysterically I might add, that this time proved over and over again to be the most precious time of the evening. It still brings a smile to the faces of my daughters and myself.

Now let's get on with sorting out the kitchen.

A basic plan that can be implemented in every kitchen:

Whether you are moving into a home and setting up your kitchen for the first time, or whether you are reorganising your current kitchen, there are many time and effort saving ideas that you will discover to turn your kitchen into a delightful place to prepare food. The style of the kitchen matters not. It is ideal to have plenty of cupboards and benchtops. However, we don't always have control over this, especially when purchasing a ready-built home or moving into a rental property.

During my lifetime, I have lived in many types of housing from a one bedroom flat when I was first married, to homes with three or more bedrooms as my children arrived. I have been privileged to live in five new homes in various locations throughout Queensland, and I have had the luxury of planning my kitchen layouts. Between locations, while waiting for each new home to be built, I have lived in various rental properties, and, during one period of my life, my husband and I even set up house with our six children in a large shed on our farm, while getting our farming venture up and running.

These days my children have all grown up and are living independent lives, and I am living in a two-bedroom unit. During all my relocations, there has been one thing in particular that I have noticed. I have developed a pattern of how I prefer to arrange my kitchen storage areas. As you can imagine, my kitchens have included different styles and sizes, and electrical appliances have changed over time, however there are basic principles which remain unchanged. I have discovered that grouping similar items close to where they are mostly used, such as storing the cookware in a bottom cupboard close to the cooktop, can save having to walk from one end of the kitchen to another. Another idea is to store bakeware close to the oven.

Some people choose to have the above benchtop cupboards with open shelves instead of with doors. They choose hooks for hanging pots and pans instead of having cupboards. This is a personal choice. Personally, I prefer cupboards with doors as I find this to be an ideal way to keep dust off the contents and the kitchen appears less cluttered. Keeping benchtops as clutter free as possible allows for extra working space for food preparation, and benchtops are easily cleaned when there are less items to move.

Clearing out the cupboards for cleaning:

Remove everything from your cupboards. It is always easier to start with a clean slate. Remove all the crockery, cutlery, utensils and glassware, pots and pans, plastic ware and bakeware. Leave the food in the pantry for now. We will deal with that later. Place everything on your kitchen table to enable a sorting process to take place. If there are items which you are sure you won't need anymore, place them aside to deal with later. A suggestion is to place them into a box to save space on the table which you will require for the items you will be keeping.

While you are removing everything from your cupboards, take note of what you can store in groups either in drawers or on shelves, and start your shopping list of any storage containers you may need to purchase. Plastic baskets and storage containers in all shapes and sizes are readily available in stores. The utensil drawer usually ends up being problematic as there are items of all different sizes, and many smaller items become lost in the maze of larger items. Another cutlery tray similar to the one in the top drawer of your bank of drawers is helpful for grouping utensils, allowing them to be visible when opening the drawer to search for a particular utensil.

Decluttering:

It is important to keep only the items you actually use. Do you have an array of kitchen gadgets that appeared as a great labour-saving idea when you saw them advertised? Then you found that they were more trouble than they were worth, and they have ended up being stashed away in the back of the cupboard and rarely used. Getting rid of clutter will make it much easier to keep cupboards tidy. If you discover that there is an item that you need to buy, purchase it now before you organise your cupboards. If you wait until later, it may be more difficult to find a good place to store it.

There are a number of ways of getting rid of items which are no longer needed. Donating to charity shops helps others, and charities are always grateful for saleable items. Garage sales are popular and can provide you with a few extra dollars to spend. Knowing that your unused items are going to a new home instead of landfill may make it easier to part with unwanted items.

Cleaning the cupboards:

Consider which cleaning products you're going to need, and, if you don't already have them, add them to your shopping list. Water soluble Eucalyptus is a wonderful cleaning product. It is available in 500ml bottles and is available at chemists and supermarkets. It has disinfectant and anti-viral properties, no nasty ingredients, smells fresh and can be mixed with warm or cold water for wiping out cupboards. Another non-chemical cleaner is vinegar diluted with a little water. A safe scrubbing agent is baking soda. There is much wisdom in choosing cleaning products that don't contain toxic chemicals, as they are much better for your health and the environment.

Clean all the dust and grime from shelves and wipe down all the doors and walls of the cupboards. To prevent mould, allow cupboard doors and drawers to remain open until all insides are completely dry. A thorough clean will help prevent bugs from entering.

If the cupboards are made from unpainted wood, take care to use cleaning agents that won't damage them. Many modern cupboards have a melamine finish that is easy to keep clean. If the cookware has left black marks on the shelves, eucalyptus solution on a cloth or paper towel will easily and safely remove the marks. Really stubborn marks will remove easily with pure eucalyptus oil on a paper towel. The oil will also remove sticky marks left behind after removing labels from jars, as well as permanent marker used to write on the sides of plastic containers to identify the contents. Before use, wash containers in hot soapy water to remove the oily residue left behind.

Unpainted shelves and drawers can be lined with butcher's paper, cork linings, or linoleum offcuts. Modern cutlery drawers usually contain a plastic type tray which has four or more sections, fits neatly into the top drawer in the bank of drawers, and can be lifted out to be washed. There are many types of trays and containers available at stores. Remember to measure your drawers before shopping. This will save numerous trips to the store.

Keeping cupboards smelling fresh:

Keeping inside cupboards clean is usually enough to keep them fresh. However, if you favour certain smells like herbs and spices, by all means use them. Small cloth bags can be made and tied or sewn securely at the top to keep dried herbs and spices in. Lavender, rose petals and cinnamon have an appealing aroma. Eucalyptus, tea tree oil and lemon oil help to keep pests away. Baking soda absorbs bad odours and can be used in cupboards as well as in the refrigerator. Replace or replenish the bags when the smells fade.

Arranging the contents:

Your cupboards are cleaned, aired and completely dry, and you have grouped similar items together. Give consideration to convenience when deciding which cupboard to use. This can save you having to walk from one end of the kitchen to the other.

THE KITCHEN

Small children:

If there are small children living in the home, store unbreakable cups and crockery on a lower shelf where the children have access.

Glassware and other breakables:

Store glassware and other breakables in cupboards above the benchtop out of the reach of children. Storing plates and dishes, which you use most often, in cupboards above the benchtop will mean you won't have to bend over to reach them.

- Place your glassware together, keeping your stemware glasses, including wine and champagne glasses, to the back of the shelf or on another shelf entirely. Place everyday glasses at the front for easy access.
- Nearby, on a shelf below the glassware for instance, store teacups and coffee mugs together for daily use.
- Place your dinnerware plates, salad plates, bread and butter plates, dessert bowls, cereal bowls and pasta bowls in a group where they are easily accessible for daily use.
- Fine china can be stored in a cupboard with a glass face if you would like to display it for decorative reasons, otherwise, store it in a top cupboard out of the reach of small hands. Store fine china cake platters which are used for special occasions near the fine china items.

THE MAGIC OF A TIDY HOME

Plasticware:

Plasticware is the cupboard which is the most difficult to keep tidy. It is best to store plasticware in a cupboard below the kitchen bench which has a top and bottom shelf. Purchase plastic baskets for lids and Tupperware seals, or use ice cream buckets, and store these baskets/buckets side by side on the top shelf. Prior to arranging the plastic containers, take a moment to match each container with the appropriate lid or seal. There is no point in keeping lids and seals if their bases are missing. Large containers with missing lids or seals can be used to store lids and seals, and they could even save you having to purchase a basket or two. Plastic magazine files are a wonderful idea for storing children's drink bottles. Bottles are usually top heavy because of the lids and tip over easily, making the cupboard look like a crashed game of skittles. If there are two or more magazine files, place them side by side on a shelf which is easily accessible to children.

- Store large containers on the bottom shelf. Similar shaped containers or sets can be stored one inside the other, with their lids or seals on their sides in a large basket.
- Store small containers on the top shelf, in the same manner as the large containers, that is one inside the other and of similar shapes. Store their lids and seals on their sides, so that all are visible, in small baskets or plastic containers. Place round shapes in one container and square shapes in another.
- Store party containers, such as Tupperware party susans, chip and dip trays, etc, which aren't used every day, at the back of the bottom shelf, complete with their seals attached so that they will easily stack one on top of the other.

Baking trays and containers:

These items are best stored in a bottom cupboard close to the oven.

- Store biscuit trays, scone trays, muffin trays and cooling racks on their sides on the bottom shelf.
- Round and square cake tins can be stacked and kept beside the trays if there is enough room or on the top shelf.
- Arrange Pyrex and ceramic casserole dishes and other ovenproof dishes and mixing bowls on the top shelf.
- Store cutting boards side by side in an easily accessible place in a cupboard of your choice for convenience.

Cookware and saucepans:

These can be stacked in cabinets under the benchtop, close to the cooktop, depending on the configuration of the kitchen cupboards. If you have a wall oven, the cupboard or drawers under the oven are a perfect storage area. These items are often heavy and awkward to stack, so it makes sense to store them where you won't have to lift them too high.

Electrical appliances:

Electrical appliances you use every day, such as the kettle and coffee maker can be kept on the benchtop. Keeping the benchtops as clutter free as possible will make cleaning much easier.

Some kitchens have an appliance cupboard with a door which opens to reveal the appliances and is complete with power points. Be aware that any appliances, such as kettles, toasters, frypans and slow cookers, which create steam, need to be used in well ventilated areas to prevent mould. It could be worth considering using these items close to the rangehood, to allow the steam to be sucked into the rangehood.

There are myriads of electrical appliances, including pancake makers, waffle irons, juicers and food processors to name a few. The pantry can be an ideal place for such items, if it is large enough and close to a benchtop.

Fancy gadgets don't work unless they are used. Keep only the appliances which you know you will use. There will always be new 'you beaut' or 'best idea ever' electrical gadgets on the market claiming to save time and make jobs easy. Some of these appliances are not as practical as they first appear to be and they can be difficult to clean.

The kitchen drawers:

Most kitchens include a bank of four drawers of similar sizes. Some even have many larger drawers that are much wider and deeper than the usual cutlery or utensils drawers, where cookware, dinner sets and the like can be stored. For the purpose of this exercise, the kitchen will have one bank of four drawers. The top drawer usually contains a plastic cutlery tray which fits exactly without room to slide around when opening or closing the drawer.
- Store cutlery for everyday use in the top drawer.
- Store utensils in the second drawer.

THE KITCHEN

- The third drawer is perfect for plastic wrap, baking paper, aluminium foil, sandwich bags, disposable gloves and items of that nature.
- The bottom drawer can be used for anything which doesn't belong on a shelf, or it could be a 'junk' drawer for all the odds and ends that have no other place to be stored. It could even be a great place to store your recipe books.

In a rental property I occupied recently, there was no cutlery tray in the top drawer, so I purchased a tray to store my cutlery. I now live in a modern unit that has a delightful kitchen with plenty of cupboards with a bank of drawers including a cutlery tray in the top drawer.

In the second drawer, I am now using the tray I formerly purchased. It measures 8cms shorter than the drawer and is the same width as the drawer. I have placed it towards the back, leaving the space at the front, where I have stored, for easy access, my longer utensils such as serving spoons, spatulas and egg lifters on their sides. My special cutlery for entertaining guests is stored in four sections of the tray, and vegetable peelers, a teacup strainer and various small items are stored in the fifth section. There is another section running widthways in front of the five sections that is ideal for storing my potato masher, whisk, kitchen shears, tongs and scrapers, all side by side. Every item is visible in the open drawer.

It is the most convenient utensil drawer I have ever used, and it happened quite accidently with the tray that I used in my former kitchen. Admittedly it has taken me a long time and many kitchens later to have such a drawer. Of course, the secret is to make sure I return each item to its original place following washing the item. Failure to do this will defeat the purpose of being tidy.

Cleaning supplies:

The best place for cleaning supplies is in the cupboard under the kitchen sink. Detergent, cleaning solutions, pot scrubbers, extra sponges and so on are located in this spot in many homes. You may require a basket or two to keep everything tidy. If there are small children in the home, a childproof door lock can prevent disasters from occurring. As some cleaning products are corrosive or poisonous, this area is not an ideal place to store food. Behind this area is an ideal location to place a cockroach bait.

The pantry:

Remove all food items from the pantry. Now is an ideal time to check the 'use by' dates on packets and cans of food, and to dispose of any items which are past the 'use by' dates.
Clean all dust and spills from shelves and wipe down the doors and walls of the pantry. Leave the doors open to air and ensure that the shelves are completely dry before placing any food back into storage. Decide how you are going to position all the items for convenience. You may wish to purchase a container for spices and another for essences such as vanilla and lemon, etc. in order to store them together, or you may already have a spice rack which could be stored on the kitchen bench close to the pantry.

If you are storing spices and essences in plastic containers inside the pantry, position the containers towards the front of a shelf at approximately waist level, so that you are able to lift then out easily in order to reach items at the back of the shelf. This shelf is ideal for icing mixture, white sugar, brown sugar, other sugars, coconut, rolled oats, flours, cornflour, various rices, and any other cooking ingredients in plastic containers or Tupperware. Label all containers with the name of the contents so that you are able to view those names without having to shuffle items around. These names are easily seen behind the lower containers of spices and essences.

The shelf above which is usually at about eye level is ideal for cans and packets of foods stacked on top of each other. Depending on how many shelves are in your pantry, lighter items such as paper towels can be stored on the top shelf. Store heavier items on the bottom shelf. The pantry contents in any household will vary, depending on how much home cooking is done and how much is stored in your refrigerator. My suggestions give you an example to enable you to make a start on a convenient storage system. You may need to make some adjustments for convenience after using your kitchen for a time. You may even wish to add some shelves which are available at stores.

The refrigerator and freezer:

The refrigerator is another food storage area and operates more efficiently when closer to full capacity. Did you know that each time the door of a near empty refrigerator is opened, there is more cold air escaping than from a refrigerator which is filled to near capacity where there is less air to escape? This can make a difference to the amount of electricity used to maintain the temperature necessary for optimum cooling performance. Items such as various flours, baking powder, chia seeds, etc. which are usually stored in the pantry, will store successful in the refrigerator door. This saves space in the pantry and reduces the amount of cold air escaping each time the door is opened.

Avoid storing leftovers unless they are going to be used within 24 hours. Ensure they are stored where they are visible. How many times have leftovers been pushed to the back of the refrigerator and forgotten about, only to be discovered weeks later in a perished state? Instead, while they are freshly cooked, place them into plastic containers, label them and pop them into the freezer. As an example, leftover cooked chicken can be frozen and later used in a salad or a curry and so on.

Before the food shopping trip, be sure to clean out the fruit and vegetable crispers in the refrigerator. Discard or compost anything that has spoiled. Cook and freeze anything that can be used in baking. For example, cooked apples are great for making apple pies. Mashed apple makes a smooth apple sauce. Mashed pumpkin is delicious in scones, cakes, pies and soups. Items that freeze without requiring cooking include bananas and passionfruit for use in smoothies, tomatoes for use in soups and dahls, to name a few examples.

The freezer is often problematic, depending on how much is stored in it. Have you ever arrived home tired after a grocery shopping trip on a hot summer's day with frozen items already starting to thaw? In your haste to get them into the freezer, they are quickly jammed into wherever they will fit. When you need them to prepare a meal, you have to remove everything from the freezer shelves to find what you want.

A simple solution to this problem is to purchase clear plastic rectangular fridge/freezer organisers which neatly fit into the freezer. Accurately measure the inside of your freezer between the shelves and write the measurements on your shopping list. Remember to include a tape measure in your handbag for use when shopping for these organisers.

Pack frozen vegetables in one storage container and meat in meal-sized portions in plastic bags in another container. Separate each piece of meat with plastic and shape into square or rectangular blocks to fit into the container with minimum space between items. Bag mince in meal sized portions and shape to fit the container. Larger items, such as bread and containers of ice cream, won't require a storage container. Store any partly used packets of food in the storage container as these boxes are harder to stack without the support of a container.

Your freezer will be so easy to manage when spending a few extra minutes during packing. A quick check in each tray when writing the shopping list ensures nothing is duplicated or forgotten, or better still, keep an ongoing shopping list with a pen in an easy-to-access place in your kitchen to list items to be replenished during your next shopping trip.

Congratulations! Job well done! You have now created magic in your kitchen. You will discover the delightful feeling of working in your tidy kitchen. Remember to return the cleaned items to their correct location to maintain the tidiness. Let's keep the magic going as we move to the bathroom in the next chapter.

THE MAGIC OF A TIDY HOME

CHAPTER 3

THE BATHROOM

Many people discover that the bathroom is the most difficult room in the home to keep clean and tidy, and the more people living in the home, the more difficult it is to keep this room so. It is the room that is used the most at one particular time of the day, mostly in the mornings when everyone is preparing to go to work and school. Being in a hurry to get out the door can result in a quick tidy up being overlooked. Have you found that dust appears to collect in the bathroom more than other rooms in the home?

Why does the bathroom trap dust?

Would you believe that the biggest culprit for dust is toilet paper? There is a paper-making science and technology called "crepe knife interaction" which is why the paper is absorbent and 'feels soft'. Every time the paper is pulled from the roll a small amount of decoupled fibre material is released, and over time you may perceive this as dust settled in the bathroom. Another culprit is the towels shedding lint that sticks to walls that are damp with steam or condensation.

The extractor fan, although highly necessary for sucking in the steam, gives the whole bathroom negative pressure and is capable of sucking in dust from the surrounding rooms as well as the dust and steam from the bathroom. In rooms with carpeted floors, dust and lint are still present, however it doesn't show as it is trapped in the carpets. Most bathroom floors are constructed with hard surface materials such as tiles, granite, etc that do not 'hide' dust and lint as well as soft surfaces.

Mould can cause serious health issues:

Mould is more likely to develop in the bathroom than in any other room in the home, therefore it is important to use the extractor fan. Many modern bathrooms, especially in high rise apartments, don't have windows, making the extractor fan more essential than ever. Good air flow throughout the whole home, especially the bathrooms, will help to conquer mould. However, more nowadays than in past times, houses are closed all day because the occupants are at work or school, and the high rate of residential break and enter is making it necessary to have everything locked up tighter than ever.

It is worth noting that bleach will not kill mould spores. Chlorine diluted with water is successful, however has to be used with caution due to safety issues which can arise from incorrectly using the product. Therefore, it is best left to a professional. Vinegar, while being a successful cleaning agent, doesn't actually kill mould spores, however eucalyptus will.

Cleaning products:

There is an array of cleaning products available in stores. In fact, the supermarkets devote a whole isle to stocking these products. With so many allergies suffered these days, many people are choosing products with more natural and less harmful ingredients. Soluble eucalyptus solution, vinegar and bi carb soda are three products that will safely take care of most jobs. It is most important to read the labels when shopping. Three quality products that come from a plant source are eucalyptus, tea tree and lemon myrtle.

Did you know that:
- Eucalyptus oil, as well as being a great cleaning product, clears nasal congestion, repels ticks, midges and sandflies, is antifungal, antibacterial and antiviral, is useful for cleaning gardening tools, kills mould spores, makes a great alternative to fabric conditioners in the laundry, just to name a few?
- Tea tree oil can be used to treat acne, toenail fungus, athletes' foot, is useful for wiping down sporting equipment, is antiviral and antifungal, makes a great disinfectant, and has many other uses.
- Lemon myrtle is a natural antibacterial and antifungal cleaner, it kills germs and mould, is a food-safe disinfectant, is safe for use on any non-porous hard surface all around the home, sanitises mops and children's toys, and the list continues…

We have covered the reasons for dust collecting in the bathroom. We have learned about the dangers of mould and why air flow is important. We have discovered some of the benefits of just a few of the many natural products derived from plants. Let's make the idea of a tidy bathroom into a reality.

Clearing the vanity unit:

Remove all contents from the shelves and drawers of the unit and wipe down all the surfaces. Wipe the outside of the vanity and leave the doors and drawers open to allow them to be completely dry before placing anything back. Spend time looking through everything to work out what to keep and where to store the items for convenience. Discard everything which has passed the use by date. If you haven't been in the habit of using storage containers to separate items into groups, take note of what requires storing and the size of the containers required. Square and rectangular shaped containers outperform round ones as they pack closer together without wasted space in between. Clear plastic or acrylic containers allow for visibility of the contents. Caddies, baskets and bins are available in many sizes in stores, and most are inexpensive.

Storing the items:

Plastic leak-proof containers are the perfect place for storing bottles of oils, liquids and anything which has the potential to leak when tipped over or when a lid hasn't been placed correctly. If a leakage does occur, it is contained to one container only, and is easily cleaned up, as opposed to a leakage occurring in an area where the whole cupboard could be affected.

Oral care:

Toothbrushes and toothpaste are commonly stored in an easily accessible place for daily use. Drawers are not ideal storage areas as brushes are damp most of the time. Use drawers to store spare toothbrushes, toothpaste, floss, etc. A wall mounted holder capable of holding numerous brushes attached above the vanity unit is ideal. Some have covers with ventilation and some even disinfect and clean the brushes. Have a look in stores and decide which is suitable for your family. Airflow to the brush bristles is an important consideration to keep in mind when deciding on a type.

Soap holders and dispensers:

These are available in all shapes and sizes and are placed close to the tap for convenience. An economical way of dispensing foam for hand washing is to purchase a refillable dispenser available at some stores. Liquid soap is added to the level on a marker on the side of the bottle, then the bottle is filled with water and shaken gently to mix as per the instructions which come with the dispenser. This is pure magic for economy.

The medicine cabinet:

Store medicines, pills, ointments, first aid kits, thermometers, dressings, bandages, etc. in a cabinet with a childproof lock on the door, and ideally out of the reach of children, completely separate from every other bathroom item. Some bathrooms have a recessed medicine cabinet with a mirrored front above the handbasin. Care must be taken when storing breakable items above handbasins to avoid accidently dropping them into the basin, resulting in broken bottles or a cracked basin.

Even supplements need to be carefully stored out of the reach of children. Many such items have been manufactured in various shapes, flavours and colours to encourage children to take them, however they are not sweets, don't always have childproof caps, and can be dangerous when swallowed in large amounts.

Makeup and beauty products:

Store makeup and beauty products where they are easily located for regular use. Remember, unlike your skin, makeup doesn't like moisture, which means, the bathroom counter really isn't the place to store it. Moisture encourages the spread of bacteria so make sure pans of blush and eyeshadow are stored in a dry place. You may even prefer to store them in a drawer in your bedroom dressing table, rather than in the bathroom. Plastic caddies and drawer dividers make life in the beauty area a breeze. Group similar items together.

Hair products:

Keep shampoo and conditioner in the shower and store spare bottles of these products in the cupboard area under the vanity. As it is more economical to purchase large bottles of shampoo and conditioner, especially when there are children living in the home, the bottles are usually quite tall, therefore they require space to stand them. Drawers are ideal for tubes of hair product, hairbrushes, clips, pins, scrunchies, ties, bands, etc. Wall mounted racks and baskets are available in retail stores for electrical grooming products such as dryers, straighteners, curling wands, etc., depending on how much wall space is available in your particular situation.

Bath towels and bathrobes:

It is best not to store bath towels and bathrobes permanently in the bathroom. Bathrooms are damp areas and often breed mould and mildew which is really difficult to get out of towels and robes. It is likely to give off a bad smell and can even make you ill. Store towels in the linen cupboard and robes in the bedroom. The complaint I most often hear about bathrooms is that there are never enough hooks and rails available for hanging wet towels, particularly in rental homes. Over the door, towel hangers can be one solution, however, be aware, that behind a door can restrict air flow and result in smelly towels. A small over the vanity cupboard door hanger is brilliant for hanging a hand towel in front of the hand basin.

Toilet brush, toilet paper holder and deodorising spray:

There are numerous toilet brush holders on the market, and I have tried them all. I find the best one is the inexpensive one available at the supermarket for only a few dollars. It allows air to get to the bristles, unlike the round variety which fits exactly into a fancy holder and doesn't allow for the air to reach the bristles. This can result in mould growth. Toilet paper holders come in all shapes and sizes. Some even have a shelf on top obviously designed to hold a mobile phone. Surely, we can go to the toilet without having to look at our phones! This is my opinion only and is said with tongue in cheek of course. Deodorising spray can be stored on the water closet section of the toilet suite, or better still, out of the reach of children, on the windowsill if there is a window in the toilet.

While speaking of the toilet, there are over the toilet storage racks available which could assist with the problem of insufficient storage space in small bathrooms, especially in rental properties where mounting items on walls is not permissible. This is a great place to store spare toilet paper, toilet deodorisers and tissues, etc. It is worth having a browse in stores that stock various types of nic-nacs.

Maintaining a tidy shower:

Where parents and children live in the home, the shower is a well-used area often resulting in a build-up of soap scum that can be difficult to remove. In order to maintain a tidy shower, dispose of any empty shampoo and conditioner bottles, leaving only presently used bottles in the shower caddy. In the shower, keep a hand towel neatly hung for airing over the shower wall and a glass window wiper for wiping down the shower walls. Introduce a rule that the last person to use the shower uses the window wiper on the glass and tiles followed by wiping down the walls with the hand towel. This could encourage the children to shower without delay to avoid having this added task after they finish showering, or ideally take it in turns to encourage them to share responsibility. The bonus for everyone is a sparkling shower with little effort, and a huge saving of time and effort removing the build-up of soap scum.

Tidy the bathroom daily:

The bathroom requires daily attention in order to maintain a tidy state. It is much easier to spend a few minutes each day than to leave it until the job becomes so huge that finding the motivation to do it becomes a challenge. When the shower is tidy, the toilet and handbasin are clean and the towels are hung to dry, there is nothing else left to do other than to appreciate the difference that just a few minutes can make.

In the next chapter we will tidy the living area.

THE MAGIC OF A TIDY HOME

CHAPTER 4

THE LIVING AREA

The living area is the most spacious area of the home and is sometimes known as the front room because it is most commonly located at the front of the home. A typical Western living room may contain furnishings such as a sofa, chairs, television, coffee tables, occasional tables, bookshelves, electric lamps, cushions and rugs. It may also function as a reception room for guests. In places with cold climates, there may be a fireplace for warmth. Very often nowadays, reverse cycle air conditioners are used to provide warmth in cooler seasons and cooling during hot summer months.

For the purpose of this book, we will be tidying a living room similar to the one in the above picture, and with the addition of bookshelves.

Let's begin with the bookshelves:

Remove the books from one shelf at a time, roughly sorting them into sizes as you proceed. Get rid of duplicate copies. Get rid of any that you know you won't be reading and any that you started reading and know you won't be finishing. Make three separate piles of books which are no longer required. The first pile will be for books to be donated to charity. The second pile will be for books that you wish to sell. The third pile will be for books that are damaged beyond repair and will be placed into kerbside recycling programs which accept magazines and paperback books as mixed paper. Some programs specifically exclude hardcover books because of the binding, unless you remove it. Check with your local program if in doubt.

There are no correct or incorrect ways of sorting books. Give some thought to what would work best for you and make a start. If you discover a better way later, simply change it at any time. You may wish to keep all the books you haven't read on one shelf and children's books on a lower shelf within reach of young enthusiasts. Another section could contain books about hobbies, such as gardening, craft, etc. Other sections could contain personal development books, true stories, fiction, and so on.

After sorting is completed, wipe down each shelf with an appropriate cloth. Microfibre is a popular cleaning cloth available singularly or in packs from stores and can be used wet or dry. Using a feather or other type of duster is not an ideal way to remove dust. In fact, all this type of duster achieves is to transfer the dust into the air where it is distributed throughout the room and has the potential to cause problems for anyone with allergies or asthma.

THE LIVING AREA

Vacuum cleaners are useful for gathering dust, particularly if they have HEPA filters. Air purifiers are worth considering, depending on your budget and available space.

Prior to returning the books to your bookshelf, it is worth testing the unit for stability. There have been instances where children have tried to climb bookshelves to reach a favourite book, and then have been pinned underneath when it has toppled over. Books are very heavy and can cause serious injuries. Brackets are available at hardware stores to fasten the unit to the wall. Repack the bookshelves according to the groups you have decided are ideal for your particular situation.

The entertainment unit:

Entertainment walls have become an important living room feature. Wall mounted TVs are replacing TVs which are placed on top of a cabinet. The sizes and features of these walls are only limited by the size of your imagination together with the size of your bank account.

Many people living in rental accommodation choose to own a TV which sits on top of a cabinet, as most landlords don't take kindly to tenants drilling holes in walls. School teachers, defence force personnel, bank managers and people who move location regularly, usually prefer furniture and appliances which are easily packed for hassle free relocation. The TV unit or entertainment unit becomes an ideal storage place for board games, card games, drawing books, colouring books and any other item which the family might enjoy together. The unit also provides the ideal area for storage of receiver and recorder equipment, plus movie media, consoles and games.

Remove all items from the unit and wipe the shelves. If a damp cloth has been used, allow the unit to remain open until completely dry. Sort everything into groups and return them to the unit. Repair any damaged board game boxes and stack them with the larger boxes placed at the bottom of the pile. Pack drawing and colouring books in a plastic basket or box. This will make it easy to carry them to where they will be used. Include coloured pencils, crayons, etc. in a separate container and store with the books in your drawing box. Smaller items such as packs of cards will remain tidy if they are stored in an appropriate plastic container. Arrange recorder equipment, movie media, etc. in a separate area in the unit.

Magazines:

Magazines can make a living room appear very untidy, especially when they are left on the lounge, sofa or coffee table. Discard any which you don't have any use for. Stack the magazines you wish to retain neatly in a magazine rack. Some coffee tables have handy shelves or drawers underneath. This is another ideal place to stack them, and, when the stack is neat, it can even add to the décor of the room by adding colour or giving a relaxed appearance to the room. When you have a collection, for example gardening or handyman magazines, etc. that you wish to refer to from time to time, a storage ottoman is a handy place to keep them out of sight, away from dust while still being easily accessible. The ottoman also doubles as a foot stool or seat or somewhere to place a bowl of popcorn while watching a movie.

THE LIVING AREA

Display items:

Paintings and family photos on walls or furniture add a personal touch to the room décor. If space is somewhat tight, maybe a floating shelf could be the solution. This type of shelf is strong while having no visible supports. It is easy to assemble as it has only two parts. It appears to float on the wall without clunky hardware or brackets. The shelf could be the perfect place for an ornament or a vase or a stylish plate or heirloom. Give your living room a cosy, relaxed appearance by adding cushions and floor rugs. This is another great way to introduce colour to brighten a neutral-coloured room.

The linen cupboard:

This cupboard is usually located in the hallway or living room. In modern homes most linen cupboards are built into the wall, with the internal area extending from ceiling to floor, while the doors are the same height as any of the doors throughout the home. The top shelf is an ideal shelf to store seasonally used items such as blankets, doonas, etc. and spares such as pillows, rugs, etc. as they can be stacked from the shelf right up to the ceiling. Prior to the modern era of built-in cupboards, furniture was mostly free standing, and many furniture pieces stood on legs or stood on the floor with a skirting board right around the bottom. Clothes were stored in free standing wardrobes, some with hanging space and a bank of drawers, and some with hanging space only. Linen was stored in a cupboard known as the linen press which usually contained only shelves.

Care must be exercised to ensure that everything that is stored in the linen cupboard is freshly washed and completely dry prior to storing it, in order to maintain freshness and prevent mould and mildew growth. Nothing encourages freshness like drying sheets and towels out in the sunshine. Sunshine also kills germs. However, many people aren't able to access this luxury as they are living in high rise apartment blocks, or in countries where there are days or weeks of damp or wet weather or extended periods of snow falls, therefore it becomes necessary to dry the washing indoors. Some homes even have drying rooms complete with airers and de-humidifiers.

Tumble driers are often used, however, be aware that a drier causes dampness in the room which can encourage mould growth. It is a challenge to dry sheets in the drier as they tend to roll up in a ball and, when they are removed from the drier, many damp spots often remain. If you must use a dryer, ensure that you air the bed linen for about an hour after removing it from the dryer. This will allow time for the fabric to breathe.

I once lived in a city which was cold and foggy during the winter months, however, I was fortunate enough to have an indoor line as well as an outdoor one. This gave me choice depending on the weather, and, these days, because my children have grown up and are living independent lives, I wash according to the weather.

In the linen cupboard, try to leave a small amount of airspace between each stack of linen, so that, each time the door is opened, air is entering the cupboard. This will prevent the musty smell which many people complain about. Lavender sachets are a great way to keep the linen smelling fresh and deter pests. Place a sachet towards the back of each shelf.

It is wise not to store linen in plastic boxes with lids, as the humid confines of plastic can encourage the growth of mould and mildew. Cardboard boxes are not recommended either, as many types of nasties are attracted to cardboard. How the linen is stored will depend on how many storage shelves are available in your linen cupboard. Store bath towels, face washers, hand towels, bathmats and hair turbans on one shelf. If space permits, store beach towels alongside the bath towels.

Some people prefer to roll towels, rather than folding them. I favour the folding method, as I find it easier to allow air space between piles. How you fold towels will depend on the depth of your cupboard. Most large towels will fit comfortably on a shelf by simply folding each towel in half, then in half again, then into thirds to form a neat flat result for stacking one on top of the other. Each towel will be visible when the cupboard door is opened. Smaller bath towels, bathmats, hand towels and face washers will stack neatly together, by stacking larger items towards the back of the shelf and smaller items in front of the larger items. Stack beach towels at one end of the shelf and bath towels at the other end.

Stack bed linen on a shelf above the towels, as it is used less frequently than the towels. For instance, bed linen is usually changed once a week, whereas towels may be changed more often to maintain freshness. Separate sheets into sizes by storing king sized sheets in one pile, queen sized in the next pile, double in another, single in another, and cot sheets, if used, in another. Fold each flat sheet to fit the depth of the shelf and fold each fitted sheet and store it on top of the matching flat sheet, so that they are in sets. A time saving tip is to print the size of each sheet on the hem with a permanent laundry marker, for example Queen, Double, etc. Be sure to fold the sheets first, to ascertain where to write the sizes so the names are easily found without having to unfold the sheets. Fold pillowcases and store them at one end of the shelf, in two piles one behind the other.

Table linen such as tablecloths, serviettes and table runners are not as popular in these modern times as they were in the past. If you have them, store them on another shelf alongside tea towels and placemats. Other items which are often stored in the linen cupboard include picnic rugs and vinyl, plastic or casual tablecloths for the barbeque table. Store chef's aprons alongside the barbeque cloths. This shelf is also ideal for storing other knick-knacks such as ham bags, used only once or twice a year, spare oven gloves and potholders.

Remember, don't throw away old clothes made from absorbent fabric that could be used as rags for polishing the car, cleaning cutlery, mopping up spills, grease rags around the barbeque or in the garage. Cut them into appropriate sizes, remove clips and buttons and store them in a drawstring bag in the bottom of the linen cupboard. Old towels have an endless number of uses, are very absorbent and can be stacked neatly beside the drawstring bag. Old sheets make great floor protectors for using under artist easels to catch the drips from the paintbrush of an enthusiastic artist. Tradespeople, such as mechanics and painters, etc. often need to purchase bags of rags for use in their occupations. Never under-estimate the value of a bag of rags. Storing the rag bag in the bottom of the linen cupboard will ensure that it is available to every member of the household at a moment's notice.

The dining area:

Formal dining rooms are not so popular in many modern homes. The dining table is often a part of the living area. As mentioned in chapter 1, for many reasons, it is very desirable for a family to spend dinner time together around the dining table and away from the TV.

In the next chapter we will tidy the rumpus/family room which could also include the dining area.

THE MAGIC OF A TIDY HOME

CHAPTER 5

THE RUMPUS/FAMILY ROOM

Are you fortunate enough to have a rumpus/family room in your home? This room is usually filled with action, and at times, can be the messiest room in the house. It needs to have the capability of being totally adaptable to meeting the needs of family members of all ages from toddlers through to teenagers. It is the ideal room for storing and playing with toys, attending to homework, practising musical instruments, building with blocks, holding indoor birthday parties in rainy weather, watching children's movies with friends, having teenage get-togethers, and the list goes on.

Being able to close the door to the rumpus/family room, so any mess isn't visible from the living room, can be a huge bonus. There is nothing more disappointing to a child who has been working hard to build an 'amazing creation', only to have to pull it to bits to tidy the room while it is still a work in progress. I am not advocating walking out of the room and leaving absolute chaos behind, as that doesn't teach children to take responsibility for being tidy, or to care for their toys. Leaving a work-in-progress in one area of the room does not have to detract from the tidy state of the remainder of the room. Of all the rooms in the home, this room requires the most flexibility regarding tidiness and order. You will notice, however, that the benefits gained from having reasonable order and being able to find what you are looking for, far outweigh the time it takes to perform a quick tidy up at the end of each day.

Take a moment to look at the picture above. A quick way to tidy this room would be to scoop the blocks into the large box, stand it upright, pop on the lid and stand the yet-to-be-completed projects on top of the lid. Place the small unused pieces back into the small box, close the lid and place it beside the large box. Park the Tonka truck beside the boxes and the room is tidy. Nothing remains on the floor for family members to trip over, while the construction project remains intact for continuation at a later time.

Let's take a look at storage available for this type of room and how to utilise it to maintain tidiness with very little effort.

Toy storage:

Toys are an important part of child development. Children spend many hours learning through play, which

helps them to develop positive attitudes toward learning. Some of the benefits include:
- Interacting with others and learning to share
- Building fine and gross motor skills
- Improving hand-eye coordination
- Learning about colours and symmetry
- Nurturing their creativity and imagination
- Becoming aware of letters and numbers for improved language skills
- Developing the senses
- Developing problem solving skills
- Learning about cause and effect.

Keeping toys in one area will prevent them from being strewn all around the home and tidiness will be easier to maintain. See-through plastic containers and baskets made from plastic covered wire make ideal storage for toys. Have separate containers for blocks, craft, jigsaw puzzles, cars, trains, Lego pieces, Barbie dolls and clothes, etc. Store the containers in open shelves for easy access. This will encourage children to participate in the tidy-up which makes your job easier and teaches them responsibility and appreciation. Perform a periodic cull to discard broken toys that aren't repairable. Outgrown toys can be given to charity or stored in a higher space for a younger sibling to grow into.

Implementing a toy rotation system can be a worthwhile exercise. Benefits include:
- Less toys are easier to pack up.
- Saves space.
- Children take better care of the toys that are out and play with them more often.
- Having less choice of toys means children are less overwhelmed.

- Children are more likely to engage in independent play for longer periods when toys are chosen to meet their interests at the time.
- Cultivates an attitude of 'less is more', encouraging them to love and care for the things they do have.
- Keeps clutter to a minimum.
- Maintains freshness and interest without having to purchase new toys.

Simple steps for rotating toys:
- Observe your child closely for a few days by keeping an eye on the toys that the child shows the most interest in, paying attention to the time span of play.
- Select the toys you feel your child may be interested in. Dispose of broken or beyond repair toys. Store for younger siblings or give away the toys your child is not fond of or are age inappropriate.
- Segregate the selection into criteria
    1. Cognitive and fine motor development – puzzles
    2. Gross motor development – balls, vehicles, trains
    3. Socio-emotional and language development – dolls, toy utensils.
- Leave the 'cannot do without' toys such as Lego, favourite dolls, a stuffed toy that acts as a security blanket, etc. out of the mix that is going to be stored for rotation.
- Write the names of the contents on each box according to their criteria.
- Empty nappy boxes make great storage boxes, as do plastic boxes with lids which clip on securely.

THE RUMPUS/FAMILY ROOM

- Store in a top cupboard out of the sight and reach of children.

An ottoman makes ideal storage for dress-up clothes, and it also serves as a seat. Dividing the room into different areas according to the previously mentioned categories, with the addition of a 'cannot do without' area for Lego, etc. is a useful way to make tidying easier. There are many ideas to assist with organising toys and each will differ according to the individual family's requirements and the size of the room. A useful suggestion is to separate the toy area from the remainder of the room by arranging a couple of cube storage shelves with closed in backs, side by side and facing towards the toys, with the backs of the units facing towards the remainder of the room. Decorate the backs with posters or artwork that your children have produced.

Homework area:

It's a good idea to set up your children in a place that has good lighting, air and enough space to spread books, pens and other resources. Younger children are more likely to work better in a family area such as the living room table, whereas older children will most likely need their own quiet space.

Wherever your children do their homework, try to minimise distractions by turning off the TV and asking younger siblings to play somewhere else. One idea is to turn homework time into a special time for the whole family to engage in quiet activities. Young children might look at books or colour a colouring book on a floor rug, while parents supervise or help the school children.

You could also ask older children to leave their mobile phones with you while they are doing homework or agree that they can't use their mobile phones or technology for social media, watching videos or playing games until the homework is complete. One exception, of course, would be when computers are required for certain homework exercises.

As previously stated, much of your child's choice of homework location depends on their ages and personal preferences. However, the bedroom is one place that is generally regarded as not ideal. This is the one place in the house that your son or daughter is most likely to be distracted and lose focus on homework. Therefore, it is probably best to keep the bedrooms off the list.

TV unit:

The TV unit adds to the amount of space available for storage in the rumpus/family room, and it can be a great place to store video games. Even if you have chosen to mount the TV on the wall, there is available space for a unit below the TV. The advantage of having plenty of storage space in this room is that it allows for less items on the floor, making tidiness much easier to achieve. This unit can also be an ideal storage place to store children's books, drawings, puzzles and board games.

Check the contents from time to time for missing, broken or damaged pieces and repair or dispose of the items. Plastic see-through containers or plastic baskets are ideal for separating items into groups.

THE RUMPUS/FAMILY ROOM

Musical instruments:

Parents who encourage their children to learn to play a musical instrument deserve full credit for outlaying the investment required to purchase the instrument. Music can be such a bonding activity for a family. I will tell you a short story from my own family. It commenced with each of my children learning to play the recorder at school. Sure, there were strange sounds to listen to, however, that was soon overcome by the look of joy on each child's face as the first tune was mastered.

My youngest daughter continued on to become what I refer to as an 'expert' at playing the clarinet. I really enjoyed listening to her playing many tunes, however, the one which stood out from the rest in my heart was "Eye of the Tiger". Thinking of her playing this piece still gives me 'goose-bumps'. She enjoyed playing with the school band and I was filled with pride each time I listened to the band play. Even after she left school, she would delight me with her musical renditions.

Now, let's return to the rumpus/family room and musical instruments. Depending on the ages of your children, it may be advisable for them to store their musical instruments in their bedrooms, away from younger children who have yet to learn the value of these instruments. Music books and stands may be stored in the same way.

In a family where the children are no longer small and maybe they are attending school, part of the room could be turned into a music area, which may even have enough space for a keyboard and drums. Then the sky is the limit as to the times that can be enjoyed together as a family or with friends.

THE MAGIC OF A TIDY HOME

When my youngest son was still living at home, he taught himself to play the guitar and drums with the help of the internet. He even soundproofed our shed at the back of our home. His friends would come over to join him in a 'music bash'. Sometimes they required a gentle reminder from me that it was 10pm, in order to show respect to the neighbours and obey the rules around noise at night. It was so pleasant to listen to the music and laughs that filled the building.

Trophies:

Over the years, children usually accumulate quite a collection of trophies and ribbons for sporting and academic achievements. Display these with pride in a display cupboard or on various types of shelving, depending on space available and the budget. The floating shelf as previously mentioned is ideal for this application.

Changing dimensions:

The rumpus/family room keeps on changing dimensions as children move from childhood to teenage years, before eventually moving out into the world to take on the challenges and joys of independent living.

The rumpus/family room is the ideal place for movie watching and eating popcorn with friends. A few bean bags and a floor rug quickly and simply take care of seating arrangements. Bean bags can be stacked to make space for a party. The list of activities in a room of this nature is endless.

This chapter has been more about suggestions, rather than actual methods of tidying. It is probably the only room in the home which requires ongoing culling and sorting at shorter intervals than any other room. Many suggestions will appeal to you and many won't. Family situations, including the number and ages of children, will vary. Use ideas that appeal to you and discard the remainder. We will all most likely agree on the importance of having a routine. When family members follow a routine, everything 'just seems to work better'.

In the next chapter, we will tidy the bedrooms.

THE MAGIC OF A TIDY HOME

CHAPTER 6

THE BEDROOMS

The Main Bedroom:

The bedroom is designated to calm and comfort you. It needs to be a place of peace and relaxation to restore your energies. It is the last thing you see before falling asleep and the first thing to greet your eyes in the morning. It is unlike the hustle and bustle areas of your home where meals are prepared, parties or gatherings take place, movies are enjoyed, and homework is completed.

The bed:

Having a comfortable bed pays dividends. Your mattress can be the difference between a good night of sleep and an unrestful night of tossing and turning, so choose the best you can afford. Ensure you turn and maintain your mattress according to the manufacturer's recommendations. This prevents sagging and wear and tear. If a new mattress isn't affordable at present, add comfort and support to your old mattress with a mattress topper.

Pillows have a lifespan and, as a general rule, should be replaced once a year, particularly if they cannot be washed in hot water. If you sleep on a lumpy, broken-down pillow, you're leaving your head and neck without proper support and you're also exposing yourself to an overgrowth of dust mites, bacteria, fungus and other allergens. Test your pillow by folding it in half and, if it doesn't return to its original shape, it's lumpy, odorous or heavily stained, throw it out and purchase a new one. You will enjoy a better night's sleep. Two or three throw pillows are perfect. More than that can be overwhelming, and your bed will be drowning in throw pillows. Donate excess to charity or rehome them to the rumpus room.

Soft sheets and a warm blanket or cover, appropriate for the season add to a restful sleep. Threadbare, torn or pilled sheets can be washed and turned into rags, to be stored in the rag bag which we created in the linen cupboard. Check your comforter or doona for odours and stains. If it is unable to be washed, replace it and cover it with a pretty one which suits your personality and the tone of the room. This is an easy way to give your bedroom a quick makeover.

Introduce peace and tranquillity into the room with soft coloured walls and furnishings. Wash sheets weekly or, at the very least, fortnightly to restore freshness and maintain a healthy environment. Fluff up the pillows and air them in the sunshine regularly. Open the windows wide and pull back the drapes each morning to allow for air circulation. Toss the sheets and covers back when first arising to air the bed before making it up for the day.

Making your bed costs nothing and takes only a minute or two each morning. It is a very powerful tool in your organisational toolbox when it comes to making your bedroom appear tidy. When your bed is rumpled and unmade, it matters not how neat everything else is. An unmade bed makes the whole room look messy. It is amazing how straightening your pillows, pulling up the sheets and smoothing out the covers can make such a difference to the room, even when other areas could use a declutter.

Lighting:

Intense overhead lighting isn't relaxing and is best left for areas such as the kitchen and rumpus/family room. Adjust your lighting to allow for bedtime reading without eye strain, dressing and night-time routines.

Sleep problems appear to be on the rise. Activities such as using your laptop in bed, playing a few games on your smartphone before sleep time or drifting off to sleep with the television on have become more common in the current age of electronic devices. Did you know that these devices have enough light to trick your brain into believing it is time to wake up, not time to relax? In fact, electronic entertainment is often stimulating enough to ward off sleep. Make it a bedroom policy that electronic devices are turned off at least an hour before bedtime. It is even better to keep them out of the room altogether. An exception could be an e-reader such as Kindle that isn't backlit.

Soft touches:

Soothing your senses will relax your mind and body, and it will introduce a peaceful environment to the room. A few candles by the bed, a bouquet of fresh flowers in a pretty vase, or a reed diffusor wafting the delicate fragrance of vanilla, jasmine, rose or lavender throughout the room, will introduce a relaxing mood. Be sure to blow the candles out before falling asleep. You may like to play soft music to drown out traffic noise or noise from a party next door. Add a few meaningful family photos, collectibles or artworks that you enjoy looking at, to add happy feelings when you look at them.

Clutter:

A messy bedroom is not a restful place. Disorganisation is the enemy of relaxation. It's difficult to switch off and drift into quality sleep when reminders of all the things you have yet to do are surrounding you. Take some time to get rid of anything you don't need or love. Return anything that belongs elsewhere in your home to its proper place. Books belong in the bookcase and magazines belong with the other magazines if you are keeping them, or in the recycle bin if you have finished with them. Get rid of anything that isn't needed, isn't loved or isn't usable.

THE BEDROOMS

Gather up any dirty clothes and place them into the laundry hamper. Take dirty dishes from bedtime snacks to the kitchen before leaving the house for the day. The bedroom is no place for items of this nature as, not only are they eyesores, but they can make the room smell, add mould spores to the air and attract unwanted insects.

Clothes storage:

Now that your room has an overall tidy appearance, it's time to sort out the contents of your storage cupboards, starting with your clothes in the hanging section of your closet. Remove one hanger at a time and lay the garments across your bed in two or three piles. One pile will be for items that don't fit or haven't been worn for a year that will be given to charity. There is no point in hanging onto clothes in the hope that they will one day fit again. This is usually an exercise in futility and a source of shame every day when you open your closet door and see them hanging there. Another pile will be for items you wish to sell or give to family members or friends. The third pile will be for the items that are to be returned to your closet. These items will mostly likely be your favourite ones that you feel comfortable in and confident when wearing.
Remove the hangers from the clothes you are giving away, then neatly fold the clothes and place them into bags. Write the intended recipients' names on each bag. Retain your favourite hangers and discard the ones that are broken or soiled. Discard wire hangers as they don't give much support to clothing shoulders and leave creases on your pants that are folded over a sagging hanger. Charities are always happy to accept clean hangers. Strong plastic and covered or uncovered wooden hangers are the

best and will give your closet a more organised and appealing appearance.

If you have enough space in your closet for winter and summer clothes, hang winter clothes at one end and summer clothes at the other. If your closet is going to be crowded, fold the clothes for the opposite season and store them in see-through plastic containers under the bed or on a top shelf or in the bottom of the closet. Containers with handles for convenient under-bed storage are available at many stores.

Group your clothes by hanging items of similar lengths together. For example, hang longer items such as dresses, pants, long coats and long skirts at one end of the hanging space, and shorter items such as folded pants, shorter coats, tops and shorter skirts next. Sturdy items like denim, cords and khakis do well folded. Use the space under the shorter items to store shoes or opposite season clothes. If you share the space with a partner, sort your partner's clothes using the same method of grouping.

Knitwear:

It is best to store knitwear neatly folded in drawers or on shelves, stacked neatly in piles that are not too high, easy to see and find. Hangers tend to stretch knitwear, whereas folding puts less stress on these garments. Wool sweaters can be stored in airtight bins, however, try not to stuff them too tightly into the bins as they need to be able to breathe properly. Cashmere sweaters do well in canvas storage bags, so they have extra breathing room and airflow. Wool and cashmere are natural fibres and will last for many years when properly cared for both with washing and storing.

THE BEDROOMS

Shoe storage:

Sort through your shoes by discarding those sandals that give you blisters, worn-out runners, stained or unrepairable shoes and unfashionable shoes that are a waste of storage space as you know you won't be wearing them again. Shoes need to be worn to last. They fall apart if they are stored for long periods without being worn. The outer skin of synthetic shoes peels off, and soles separate from shoes as the glue disintegrates.

Shoes are best stored in their original boxes and is the optimal long-term storage area. Storing them in the box protects them from the damages caused by sunlight, dust and extreme temperatures. The ends of many boxes display a picture of the shoe within. If not, write with a marker the name and colour on the end of the box, for example 'black flatties' or silver sandals with heals', etc., to avoid having to open the boxes to identify the contents. Stack them with the larger boxes at the bottom of the stack with the name facing towards the front.

Always air your shoes for a few hours or overnight before storing to allow odours to escape and dampness to dry to avoid mould issues and keep them fresh. Cleaning shoes prior to storage will help prolong their life. Retain the sachets of moisture absorbing crystals that are contained in the original box. Remove tissue paper from any boxes as silver fish are attracted to this type of paper. Some of the more expensive shoes come wrapped or bagged in soft fabric inside their boxes. Plastic boxes can be purchased for less expensive shoes that often don't come in boxes.

Shoes made from natural materials like leather and suede will last longer than ones made from synthetic materials. Leather costs more, however, it is worth paying extra for.

Polish them regularly to condition and protect the leather, and, if you have worn them in the rain, allow them to dry completely before wearing them again. Unlike shoes made from synthetic materials, leather shoes breathe and spare you from embarrassing foot odour. Avoid storing leather shoes in plastic boxes as they can mildew.

Socks and underwear:

Do you have a 'lonely socks club' in a box or bag in the laundry or in a corner or drawer in your bedroom? No one knows for certain where individual socks disappear to, but they leave behind lonely mates. Hold onto single socks for a week or two in case the missing sock reappears, but beyond that, the lonely socks take up space for no good reason. If some are suitable for household cleaning, store them in the rag bag, and toss the rest.

Store the wearable socks in a drawer with dividers that can be made using plastic ice cream containers or plastic baskets that fit neatly into the drawer without wasting space. Fold socks together in pairs to avoid adding to your 'lonely socks club'. Hosiery can be stored in the same drawer if space is available. Thick work socks may require a separate drawer.

Fold or roll knickers neatly and arrange at the front of a drawer side by side so each one is visible when opening the drawer. There will be plenty of space behind the knickers to store support underwear. Depending on the size of your drawers, you may need to store bras in another drawer. Store padded bras one in front of the other and close together on their lower edges to avoid folding them and altering their shape. Unpadded bras can be folded one cup inside the other and straps tucked into the cups for storage.

Where possible, store similar items in groups. If you have more shelf space than drawer space, items that would usually be stored in drawers can easily be stored in see-through plastic containers or baskets on the shelves. Much depends on how much storage space you have available when it comes to placement of clothing.

Bedside storage:

Bedside storage units with drawers are a practical way to add to your storage space. Table-style nightstands may add a touch of beauty to the bedroom however they are not practical storage solutions. Drawers create space to stash the sundries that tend to clutter up the bedside area, items such as tissues, lip balms, pen and paper, hand creams, and any items you may require that you would otherwise have to get out of bed to find. Keep a journal and pen in your drawer for those times when inspiration strikes or when you remember something important you almost forgot about. If you are a bedtime reader keep your book or Kindle reader in a drawer. When items are readily available without having to get out of bed after retiring for the evening, you are more likely to relax and drift into peaceful sleep.

An attractive bedside lamp on each bedside unit serves as a useful light for bedtime reading and adds to the décor of the room. Add a small photo or ornament and aim to keep the top of the unit clutter-free to enhance the tidy appearance of the room and make dusting easier. If you share the room with a partner, you will have a bedside storage unit each.

Dressing table:

The top of the dressing table can become a dumping ground for all sorts of bits and pieces, even the laundry you just folded. Form a habit of spending a few minutes to put folded laundry away as soon as you have finished folding. Keep the top of the dressing table clean and tidy at all times by avoiding the tendency to overcrowd the space available. Less is more. Keep it simple. If you apply your makeup at the dressing table, a pretty bottle of perfume could be one item you might display, along with some makeup items on an attractive tray and a makeup mirror. Other examples are a couple of small photos, a vase of flowers, an ornament or a jewellery box.

The dressing table with drawers can be turned into a pamper centre. Place suitable sized plastic containers in the top drawer to protect the furniture from spills and separate various makeup items, oils and perfumes, etc. into groups. Store scarves in another drawer, jewellery in another, and so on. Keeping all these items together allows for convenience when meeting deadlines for work and social engagements.

More storage space:

Install hooks on the back of your bedroom and closet doors, and use them to hang your bathrobe, purse, hats and belts. Depending on the size of your bedroom, there may be enough room for a storage box at the foot of the bed. Adding a padded seat pad to the top provides a convenient place to sit while pulling on your shoes in the morning. Be careful not to have it become another place to dump clutter.

THE BEDROOMS

Can you ever have too much storage space in the bedroom? Not really, providing that you are diligent about getting rid of clothes and items that no longer serve you. Bedrooms should be home only to those items you truly love. If you are keeping collectibles that are past their glory days, it's time to get rid of them. This will free up space in your room and in your mind.

The Children's Bedrooms:

Take a look at the picture above. Wouldn't it be wonderful if it would remain that way? Well, we all know that it won't. Gather up a dozen parents and ask them what their main complaint is when it comes to their children's bedrooms, and the most common reply you will hear will go something like, "It looks like a tornado hit it." Most children are not usually natural-born organisers. In fact, many appear to revel in a huge mess.

However, children learn what they live and live what they learn. When the parents are tidy, children have an ideal to follow. When the parents are untidy, the children follow an example of untidiness. We do our children a favour by teaching them organisational skills at an early age. An untidy bedroom can be a safety issue, and good habits learned early are likely to stay with them for a lifetime.

Regardless of their ages, the secret to well-organised children's bedrooms is providing plenty of clearly defined storage areas throughout their rooms. Without obvious places to store their possessions, most children will simply leave their belongings on the floor or shove them under the bed or into the closet. To help children learn good habits, provide them with easily accessible storage spaces, and take the time to teach them how to use them.

Safety:

Safety is an important issue throughout the home as a whole, however, it is even more important in the bedrooms of smaller children. They love to climb, have a tendency to act on impulse and have no idea about safety. Therefore, it is wise, and can be a life-saving factor, to take a serious look at safety features.

Properly fitted security screens on windows will prevent your toddler from climbing up and falling out when something outside has caught his/her attention. We don't want toddlers getting outside without supervision and wandering onto the street. A window stopper could be installed so that the window can partly open. Care must be taken to ensure airflow that is important for cooling and mould prevention is not restricted. If you live in a residence without screens, window guards could be worth checking out.

Avoid accidents where children have become tangled in cords from vertical drapes, blinds and curtains. Modern versions of these are fitted with child-safe opening and closing devices and vertical drapes are now made without the plastic chains between the weights at the bottom of the drapes, but it is likely that older ones won't be.

Furniture items must be secured to the wall to prevent them tipping over and landing on your child. You never know when a child might decide to climb to reach something at the top. Furniture might appear sturdy enough to stay put, but when your toddler climbs up on it, his weight added to the front is often enough to pull the whole thing forward and down on top of him/her. Furniture wall straps are one way to make sure that furniture is secure.

Care should be taken to remove choking hazards to protect your own toddler as well as visitors' children. Be aware that children may try to poke things into the power outlet. In most countries these days, safety switches are installed in the meter box by the electrician and will immediately trip the switch to cut the power. Plug covers for power outlets are another idea, but it doesn't take children long to learn how to remove them. They watch everything we do and try to copy. Try to hide cords for lamps, etc. behind furniture or use a wire guard to prevent lamps being pulled over and falling on the child's head. Safety gates in doorways and at the top and bottom of stairs are useful.

Children's beds:

When children are old enough, encourage them to make their beds every morning. Resist following them around to straighten the covers and pillows. They will improve as they practise the habit. Bunk beds can be a challenge even for an adult, especially when we are rather short in stature. Giving smaller children some margin will encourage them to keep trying, and they will be less likely to give up. Straighten the cot sheet, arrange the soft toys and fold the blanket to tidy the cot.

Clutter:

At the beginning of each season, sort through children's clothes, and pass on, give to charity or store in a plastic container for a younger sibling, any items they have outgrown. There is no point in clogging up storage space with clothes that don't fit.

I have fond memories from when my children were young. We made a game of trying on the clothes from the previous year. We were always amazed at how much they had grown during the time between one year and the next and enjoyed many laughs. The legs of the long pants ended just past their knees. The sleeves of their tops barely came past their elbows. Buttons wouldn't button up. Shoes wouldn't fit. My children delighted in how much they had grown, and it was a fun way of clearing out the hanging space and the drawers to get rid of clutter.

Clothes storage:

Hang clothes according to their length in the closet. If two children are sharing a bedroom, separate the clothes and, where possible, use hangers in different colours, one colour for each child. When a child is very young, the hanging rod needs to be low enough for the child to be able to reach it. If that is not possible, it is best to fold everything and place the clothes into drawers.

Fold any clothes that don't hang and store them in drawers, using top drawers for the older child and lower drawers for the younger child so that they are within reach of each child when learning to dress themselves and when they are packing clean clothes away.

The dressing table or chest of drawers:

A dressing table with plenty of drawers or a chest of drawers is ideal for pyjamas, underwear, socks and tee shirts. Start teaching your child to place clothes neatly into drawers as soon as he or she is old enough to understand your directions. Use pictures to label each drawer with the contents. On laundry day, encourage your child to place the clean, folded clothing into the appropriate drawers. Young children enjoy such activities, and it will encourage the habit to last when the fun is outgrown.

Older children won't need labels but may need assistance in deciding the best way to group clothing items in the drawers. Give help as required, and on laundry day, a reminder may be required to put his/her clean clothes into the appropriate drawers.

Shoes:

Store shoes in the bottom of the closet, again separating the storage area for different ages. Encouraging children to put their shoes away and keeping them in pairs will spare you and them from having to hunt for that missing shoe when time is at a premium, for instance when needing to get to school on time or catching a bus.

THE BEDROOMS

Large trunk or storage box:

Because this is an item that's going to be used for years, choose a design that works with the bedroom design and is suitable for all aged children, preferably made from wood, not plastic that usually splits. Ensure that it has safety latches that prevent the lid from slamming down on little fingers or locking a hiding child inside.

Even when toys are stored in a family/rumpus room, there can still be a place in their bedrooms where they store items of a more individual nature. Perhaps there is a favourite doll or stuffed toy or truck, for instance, in the early years, and, as they move through the school years, the items will switch to games, art and craft supplies and the like. During preteen and teen years, the storage box can be put to good use holding sporting equipment, electronic games, school supplies and musical instruments.

Shelving units:

Children's bedrooms need plenty of shelves that can be bookcases, open-backed shelving units, or shelves mounted on the walls. Shelves don't need to be fancy, as long as they are secure enough that they don't tumble if a young child decides to climb on them. An old bookcase from another part of the home or a charity shop painted a bright colour would be ideal.

Provide lots of baskets or plastic see-through boxes with lids to fit neatly side-by-side on the lower shelves. When children have adequate storage containers, they are more likely to want to tidy their spaces. As children grow, you may be able to dispense with some of the baskets, however ample storage will always remain an important part of a tidy bedroom.

As their interests change, the need for storage will remain high as they will require places for beads, other small craft supplies, paint, markers and small toys. These may be unsuitable for storing in the rumpus/family room where some items could pose a danger to visiting children who may not be aware of your family rules regarding the care and use of these toys. Teens will probably fill the open shelves with books and collectibles, and they may prefer to keep their trophies in their bedrooms rather than in the rumpus/family room.

The laundry hamper:

Provide a laundry hamper for each bedroom and encourage children to place their dirty clothes, including socks, into it as they undress. Stress to them that tossing wet towels into the hamper is an 'absolute no no' because of the serious issue of mould forming on unaired towels.

Under–bed storage:

One or two large see-through plastic under-bed storage boxes always come in handy for extra storage space. Personalise the boxes by writing each child's name on his/her box and encourage children to tidy their respective boxes regularly. Depending on the ages of your children, these boxes are perfect for holding out-of-season clothing, large drawing paper pads, artwork, sporting equipment, odd collections children enjoy and even an extra rug or snuggle blanket easily accessible for cooler days or nights.

THE BEDROOMS

Even with all of the spaces and containers you provide, your children might not always keep their bedrooms to your expectations. However, the odds are much more favourable when they have easy access to storage, and an occasional gentle reminder. Giving encouragement with compliments here and there for jobs well done demonstrates to them that you have taken notice and appreciate their efforts.

In the next chapter, we will take care of the working areas, including the office, the sewing area and the art area.

THE MAGIC OF A TIDY HOME

CHAPTER 7

THE WORKING AREAS

The Office:

Your office may be a closet door that opens to reveal a number of built-in shelves, one of which slides out to form a desk for your laptop, phone, an in-tray, a desktop unit of drawers for printer paper, sticky notes, notebook, diary and a pen. A comfortable chair is tucked under the desk, plastic see-through containers store your office necessities such as a stapler, sticky tape, pens, pencils, paper clips, rulers, a hole punch, and so on.

If you operate a business from home, you may have a whole room for your office at the front of your home. A tradesman's business, for example, may have a large desk with shelves or a bank of drawers attached, a filing cabinet and one or more comfortable chairs, especially if clients or sub-contractors attend your office for various reasons.

Maybe you have combined your office with other activities, such as artwork, sewing and craft. In that case your office furniture may be arranged in one area of the room and your sewing gear or artwork in another. If you sew you may have furniture appropriate for storing materials, patterns, craft items, a sewing box for threads, scissors, tape measures, pins and needles, for example. If you enjoy art activities, such as drawing, painting and sketching, you may have an artist easel, and furniture for storing your paints, pencils, brushes and sketch pads, just to name a few of the endless supply of items that find their way from the art supplies shops to the artist's home.

Maintaining tidiness in the office can present challenges, especially when the office is shared with other activities such as sewing and art. Therefore, we are going to sort this out by working through one area at a time, and you will be amazed at how simple it can be. Let's make a start with the office area.

The idea of a paperless office was born in 1975 when a Business Week article predicted offices would become paperless after the first computer terminals were introduced. Although these days computers are commonplace, so are home offices with filing cabinets and printers. Therefore, this exercise includes some items that may be disposed of sooner or later. We certainly have moved into a digital age and many offices, including home offices, have embraced the new mode of operation.

THE WORKING AREAS

The office desk:

It is essential to have a workspace that's organised and relaxing to work in. When your space is neat and tidy, you will notice your mind is clearer, and your productivity improves. A cluttered workspace equates to a cluttered mind, resulting in stress and anxiety. Taking these few simple steps to tidy this area will conquer these problems. Ensure you have trays, dividers and containers on hand to separate and store your items. A waste-paper bin close to where you sit is a necessity in any office and it will make tidying up a whole lot easier.

- Determine what items, paperwork and supplies you really need and what you can do without. Take a good look at what you have on your desktop and in your storage areas. Sort into different piles, one for items you use daily, one for items you use occasionally, and one for items you never use.
- Wipe down the desktop with a dampened cloth, microfibre is a great dust remover. Wipe the dust from the drawers and shelves and allow them to dry thoroughly. Electro-statically charged cloths that actually attract dust are available and are handy to have around the office for quick dusting jobs.
- Sort through the pile of items you use daily. Place pens and pencils together in a desk top caddy or in a tidy tray in the top drawer of your desk, alongside the usual items such as paperclips, staples, scissors, rulers and sticky tape, and so on.
- Sort the items you occasionally use into categories, place them neatly into containers and store them where they are accessible and aren't taking up

space on your desk. The second drawer may be the answer.
- Separate the items you never use into two piles, one to give to charity and the other to dispose of. If you have a shredder, wastepaper can be shredded and added to the compost bin.
- Simply hiding as many cables and cords as possible will make a huge difference to how clean and tidy your workspace appears. Ensure that your cords are accessible without drawing too much attention to them.
- A surge protector is useful to protect your computer from power spikes, especially in areas prone to storms and other unstable weather events.
- Develop the habit of tidying your desk at the end of each day to ensure that you always have a clutter-free desk. It only takes a few minutes to return items to their storage places to promote a positive start to each workday. No more time will be wasted looking for misplaced items.

The filing cabinet:

The two-drawer filing cabinet is usually the same height as a desk and the top of the cabinet makes an ideal place to store the printer. You may discover that you only need to use the top drawer as hanging file numbers reduce during your transition to becoming paperless. The bottom drawer becomes available for extra storage of items other than hanging files. Save time by filing your current archived papers in a box that fits into the drawer. Each year after lodging your tax return, you will dispose of the archive from five years prior to the current year, until the archive box eventually becomes empty. If the time comes when you no longer require a filing cabinet and printer, simply discarding both items will increase space in the office.

Digital filing:

Even when files are kept in digital form, the need for proper record keeping and archiving remains. Ensure that you have a reliable system and keep everything up to date on a regular basis. Keeping your computer clutter-free is no less important than keeping physical space clutter-free. Attend to emails daily to prevent a build-up becoming overwhelming. Unsubscribe from senders of emails that are of no interest to you. Remember to keep your daily reminders up to date to avoid missed engagements.

The office chair:

Extra care should be taken when choosing a suitable office chair. It needs to support your back to minimise back ache and bad posture. Taking into account how much time you are going to be spending at your office desk will give you a guide to a suitable chair that fully meets your requirements. The chair that glides around effortlessly on five smooth running castors, as opposed to the budget chair with only four castors, is well worth the extra cost incurred. The office chair, particularly one without arms, is also suitable for use in the sewing area. Simply roll from one area to the other.

There are as many good reasons for investing in a chair mat as there are types of mats available.
Reasons include:

- Protects hard floors, including wood, tile, linoleum and vinyl from indentations, scuffs and scratches
- Protects carpeted floors from wear and tear, dirt and stains
- Makes it easier to move within your workspace
- Takes 80% less effort to roll your chair on a mat than on carpet
- Promotes less back pain and leg strain.

Types of mats include:
- Polyvinyl chloride (PVC) is light, thin and cheap, and is a good option for light home office use. It is suitable for hard floors and low pile carpet.
- Polycarbonate is a strong and durable material that can take heavier weights and more frequent use. It is suitable for all types of floors and all types of carpets.
- Tempered glass is the most durable and the most expensive of the three types. It is eco-friendly and will outlast several plastic mats. It is suitable for all types of floors and all types of carpets.

It is well worth the time and effort required to speak with an expert in the field of office mats before purchasing one as there are many points to consider in order to prolong the life of the mat. Bottom surfaces of mats include smooth, cleated and spiked and each has different applications for different flooring.

I recently experienced a situation in my office/sewing room where a chair mat came to my rescue. I encountered a challenge with the section of my sewing machine cabinet that contained my overlocker and a couple of drawers. When I rolled this heavy section out, the castors became stuck in the soft vinyl floor covering. Persistence would have caused damage to my cabinet as well as the floor covering, however, the challenge was easily overcome with a chair mat that was large enough to protect the floor area under the sewing cabinet and allowed the castors to move easily. Because my office desk was against the nearby wall, the chair-mat served both my office desk and my sewing cabinet, and I was easily able to roll from one area to the other.

You may discover that you can utilise one chair-mat for two areas. Much will depend on how many people work in your room at the same time. If there are two people, you would have two chairs and this wouldn't work, however, this is a tip that is worth some thought. This now brings us to the sewing area.

The Sewing Area:

The sewing area can be as simple as a place to hold a sewing machine and a sewing box containing the bits and pieces required to perform a few simple tasks, or it can be an elaborate set up with a specially designed cabinet for the sewing machine, an overlocker and sewing bits and pieces. Much will depend on whether you sew for pleasure or whether you engage in income producing sewing such as dressmaking or alterations for others. You may have a cabinet for fabrics, patterns and sewing paraphernalia, as well as a cutting table and dressmaker's model.

The specially designed sewing cabinet that folds out to form a cutting table and opens up to reveal a pop-up shelf for the sewing machine and a pull-out area on castors for the overlocker and a set of drawers, requires enough floor space for the cabinet when it is fully opened. This equates to four times the depth of the cabinet, as you would be aware if you are fortunate enough to own one of these amazing cabinets.

I was blessed with a grandmother who was a talented dressmaker. She sewed clothes for many satisfied clients throughout the district and happily worked in a small room that her son-in-law had converted into a sewing room by building in a section at the end of the front veranda of her home. She used her sewing machine positioned on a cabinet. Nearby she had a cutting table and a storage place for her dressmaking paraphernalia. As you can imagine, this room was always a busy place, however Grandma was always organised. She had a place for everything and kept everything in its place. Whenever I observed her while she was sewing, she always knew where to locate any item she needed. She would arrange each client's fabric, together with a packet containing the necessary extras such as a zipper, buttons, thread and decorative items, into a neat pile in a designated area and repeated this action for each subsequent client. Her example was a valuable lesson in tidiness for me to follow with my sewing. I will now work with you to tidy your sewing area, and you will be able to easily locate your items as well. Let's get started.

The sewing machine space:

You may have a sewing cabinet with drawers on one or both sides of the space where you sit on an adjustable chair to operate the sewing machine, or you may have a specially designed cabinet as described in a previous paragraph with a top drawer that comes with a divider similar to that of a cutlery drawer only on a smaller scale, or even a small table where you remove the sewing machine from its carrier bag and use it on a table.

If you don't have drawers for storage, purchase one or two sewing boxes that are designed to hold sewing equipment and accessories. Many boxes have trays that lift out or fold out, allowing storage of items such as thread, buttons, marking chalk, spare machine needles, bobbins, seam rippers, safety pins, thimbles, threaders, bodkins, seam gauges, soft tape measures, straight pins, needles and so on in small compartments. Most boxes have a carry handle on the hinged lid, to avoid tipping the box to carry it, thus allowing the contents to remain in place.

The following items require extra care when storing to prevent damage to the item and the user:
- Bent handle shears/dressmaking shears are a sewer's best friend. Store them in the slip pouch they usually come in from the manufacturer to protect the blades. Keep them out of the reach of children. These shears are strictly to be used only for cutting fabric. Paper and leather will cause the blades to become blunt. Shears are truly a case of getting what you pay for, and every expensive pair is well worth their price tag.
- Regular straight scissors are used for cutting patterns and paper. Remember not to cut plastic with these as it can dull the blade quickly and make cutting patterns difficult. Keep these out of the reach of children too.
- Embroidery scissors are great for snipping off threads that remain when a sewing project is completed on a sewing machine and when you start and finish a line of stitching. They are designed with fine points for intricate tasks. Dropping them onto a hard surface floor will damage the points and render them useless for fine tasks. Again, keep them out of the reach of children.

Store the tools that come with your sewing machine in an accessible place such as the top drawer, together with a clip-on magnifying glass for close-up work and a desk lamp, particularly useful for sewing dark-coloured fabrics.

The sewing/craft cupboard:

As you remove each item from your storage cupboard, organise them into piles. Place items you know you won't use into one pile, and everything else into a separate pile each for fabrics, fabric scraps, patterns, elastics, zippers, ribbons, bindings, decorative items such as braids, laces and motifs, and sundries.

Wipe the shelves and allow them to dry. Fold the fabrics into uniform sizes that will fit neatly on a shelf to conserve space and be visible when the door is opened. Stack one on top of the other until the pile reaches the underside of the shelf above. Repeat this until all fabrics are stored. Fold fabric scraps that are large enough to make small items such as younger children's pants and tops and store next to the stored piles. Place small scraps into a large plastic container for use as trimmings, craft ideas such as quilting and so on.

Sewing patterns are best stored in a large plastic box with a lid. Many patterns are made from tissue paper that attracts silver fish, so it is best to fold them and place them back into the paper packet they came in and use clip-lock plastic bags for protection against pests. Store elastics, zippers, ribbons, bindings, decorative items such as braids, laces and motifs in a suitably sized see-through plastic container or a sewing box.

In order to maintain tidiness in the sewing area, flexibility is required during a particular sewing job, in order to survive the chaos of having bits of material and thread everywhere, the ironing board nearby, patterns out of their box and electrical cords running here, there and everywhere. This is only a temporary situation, however, until the sewing jobs have been completed and everything is packed away.

Depending on the size of your cupboard and the size of your ambition, there may be enough space to store requirements for your many other interests, such as scrap booking, beading, knitting, crochet and so on, or you may even store some or all of them in another space. Staying organised means giving serious thought to planning your space. You'll be amazed at what can be achieved within just one room when giving careful consideration to the result you wish to see.

It is important to separate everything into categories. Knitting yarns store well in fabric draw-string bags or plastic bags or bins. Store balls of crochet thread in plastic containers with lids. Stack knitting and crochet patterns together in a suitably sized plastic container with a lid. Store knitting needles, stitch markers, row counters, darning needles and crochet hooks together in an appropriate container with a lid. Store scrapbooking albums and paper on a shelf and tools in a plastic container. Small items and embellishments are often stored in clear glass jars allowing you to know at a glance what you have available. Adhesives, scissors, trimmers and cutters require storage with the safety of small children in mind. A higher shelf is ideal for this application, ensuring that categories are maintained.

THE WORKING AREAS

Depending on the types of interests you enjoy, either through necessity for income purposes, or as part of your leisure activities, life will be so much more productive and enjoyable when regular order is maintained to make the most of the 24 hours each day that is given to all of us. I am now going to mention another activity that many of you may enjoy and that is in the world of art.

An artist who is heavily engaged in this activity may be fortunate enough to have a separate art room or studio. However, if art is something you enjoy dabbling in from time to time, a small space in the office might be all you require.

The Art Area:

Activities such as the one in the above picture can be completed in a small space by using the cutting table in the sewing area or by using the office desk. Storage space could be a shelf in the sewing/craft cupboard, or it could be a unit with shallow drawers. Grouping items together, similar to the method established in other rooms in your home, will make it less likely for items to be misplaced and much easier to maintain tidiness.

Depending on space available and your budget, the most convenient and practical way of storing art supplies is in shallow drawers. This avoids the need to stack items on top of each other and you will see at a glance what you store in each drawer. Units with shallow drawers are readily available with or without castors, in a variety of sizes, ranging from five to seven drawers. They are space savers that fit under desks or in closets where they are out of traffic areas. Drawer organisers that vary in prices and sizes are ideal for storing pencils, brushes, erasers and so on. Store boxes of pastels, mixing palettes, fixative, paper and so on in drawers that don't require drawer organisers.

Vertical storage is a great storage method when there is limited floor space and available wall space. Hang a pegboard or two on the wall and let your imagination take over. Many types of storage containers, hooks and attachments are available for pegboards, and having visibility of all items from paintbrushes and pens to scissors and tapes and so on is a time saving bonus for the up-and-coming artist. Placing a shelf above the pegboards creates an ideal place to store art books, paper and sketch pads and everything is visible at a glance.

Store some old sheets in the bottom of the cupboard or in a bottom drawer to be used to protect the floor if necessary. A bag of rags is useful for cleaning up spills, paint brushes and so on, as are paper towels.

In the next chapter, we will tidy the garage and the garden shed.

THE MAGIC OF A TIDY HOME

CHAPTER 8

THE GARAGE AND GARDEN SHED

The Garage:

Is this what happens at your home? Is your car parked out on the driveway as there is no space in your garage because it contains everything except the car? There are boxes of 'stuff' everywhere, tools, sporting equipment, car care equipment, children's bicycles and the list builds. The garage often ends up being a dumping ground for so many items that you just want to stash away somewhere out-of-sight, out-of-mind. Relegating them to the garage and closing the door is a temporary fix and works until the time arrives for you to find something.

Decluttering:

Let's end this daunting situation by starting with decluttering. Go through everything in your garage and sort it into three piles, one for items you wish to keep, one for donating or selling and one for items to dispose of. Organise all the items you are keeping into categories such as handyman tools, camping gear, sporting gear and so on.

Observe your categories and plan how you are going to store them. Let's take a moment to give some thought to different types of storage:
- Overhead storage is ideal for storing items that are used seasonally or only occasionally. It is a great way to keep things off the floor and out of the way. When hanging shelves from the ceiling, check to ensure the garage door has enough space to function properly and higher vehicles will fit under the shelf.
- Open storage shelves, as opposed to cabinets, will do away with having to allow extra space for cabinets doors to swing open, thus limiting the amount of usable floor space. Clear plastic rectangular shaped containers with lids will fit easily on the shelves and you'll be able to quickly see all the items you have stored. If you aren't able to close the door on mess, you'll be less likely to hide things behind a door, and more likely to be motivated to maintain tidiness.
- Pegboards and hooks are perfect for hanging frequently used items, such as hand tools. A shelf above the tool pegboard could be the perfect place for a twenty-drawer compartment organiser

- with clear plastic drawers that allow the contents to be viewed at a glance to store nails, screws, bolts, drill bits, hooks and so on. It would be safely out of the reach of small children, and easily accessible when you need to hang that painting or put up that curtain track. Nails and screws would be carefully kept away from car tyres.
- Slatwall panels are grooved panels that attach to the wall and are commonly used when fitting out shops. They are worth considering for a garage wall as they allow different kinds of baskets, hooks, brackets and shelves to be attached to the grooves. This could be a space-saving way to hang brooms, ladders, power leads, and so on.

Measuring and planning:

Measure your garage and draft a floor plan, paying particular attention to available wall space and ceiling space. Our aim with garage storage is to clear the floor space of as many items as possible. This makes cleaning easier and protects items from water drips when driving your car into the garage during rain.
- Note the length and number of shelves required
- Note brackets and screws for the shelves
- Calculate the number and sizes of clear plastic containers with lids required
- List the twenty-drawer compartment organiser
- Note any baskets and hooks required
- On the way to the shops, swing by the charity store to drop off any items destined for donations.

When your construction project is complete, sweep or vacuum the shelves and floor and give yourself a pat on the back for a job well done. It is time now to pack your items into their various places.

Tools:

Hang your handyman tools neatly on the pegboard. Remember to return them to their respective places after use. Store power tools on the shelf above the peg board along with the twenty-drawer compartment organiser, spirit level and so on.

Camping gear:

Storing all your camping gear together makes packing for a trip quick and easy. It lessens the likelihood of arriving at your destination to discover something has been left behind. Keep a small hammer or mallet permanently with your camping gear for hammering in tent pegs. This is one item that is most often forgotten when setting off on a camping trip.

Group similar items together in separate clear plastic containers with lids, for example meal preparation items such as pots, pans, utensils, cutting boards, etc. in one container, meal serving items such as plates, bowls, mugs, cutlery, paper towels, etc in another container and so on.

After a camping adventure always clean and air your camping gear on arriving home and ensure it is thoroughly dried prior to storage. This will maintain it in good condition, prevent mould and prolong its life.

Picnic and barbeque gear:

As picnics and barbeques with friends and family usually occur more frequently than camping trips, it is probably more appropriate to store portable coolers, known as eskies in Australia, chilly bins in New Zealand, coolers in the USA, cool boxes in the UK, insulated water bottles, picnic blankets and baskets in an easier-to-reach place, on a shelf next to the sporting equipment for example. Folding chairs need to be easily accessed as they are often used in many situations including picnics, barbeques and watching children's sporting events. Many chairs are in bags that will hang on hooks on walls or poles.

Bicycles:

There are literally dozens of ways of storing bicycles, however, it all depends on how much space is available and how much the budget is able to stretch. Bicycles take up a lot of floor space. They can easily be hung, depending on the type of bicycle. Care must be exercised with some types, for example mountain bicycles with hydraulic brakes hung vertically will facilitate air transfer into the system thereby making the brakes spongy. Remember to pump the brake lever for some time prior to riding.

Hanging vertically by the front wheel is the most space efficient way to store a bicycle. Rubberised hooks are available in many shops. Racks are also available that allow 3 or 4 bicycles to be stored side by side, however more space is required when mounting the rack on the wall. The space benefits of hanging bicycles vertically far outweigh any other method of storing them.

Store tools and spare parts for the bicycles in a plastic container with a lid on a shelf near to where the bicycles are stored. There are many types of racks, hooks, stands and bags for storing bicycle helmets, depending on your budget and the level of importance cycling holds in your life. The most important thing with children's helmets is to encourage children to take care of their helmets by not leaving them outside in the weather.

I noticed a clever idea recently in the form of a shelf on the wall, that had hooks for bicycles on the under-side and plenty of space on the shelf top for helmets and locking devices.

Sports equipment:

Sort your gear by sport rather than piling it all together in one place. This will save you time as well as help you remain organised, especially on those Saturday mornings when your children are gathering their equipment to get into the car for the trip to the sports field.

Once the gear is sorted, use shelves to hold large items such as helmets and skates, sporting bags containing hockey sticks, cricket bats, protective pads, helmets, gloves, etc. Use wire baskets to hold small equipment and mesh laundry bags for tennis balls, shuttle cocks, etc. Store outgrown sports shoes that are to be passed onto a younger sibling in wire baskets or side by side in pairs on a shelf to enable airflow to prevent mould and odours.

Fishing gear:

There are many great ideas for storing fishing rods from wall mounted racks and hooks to ceiling mounted attachments. I am sure that if you are a person whose love is fishing you will have a number of rods and will know the best way to store them to ensure that hooks don't end up in children's feet, tackle boxes are in child safe places, while at the same time, taking care of your pride and joy.

Car care gear:

Store the car wash products in a plastic bucket on a shelf where it will be readily available for a quick wash. Store products used for a more detailed clean, such as polish, tyre black, etc. in a plastic container next to the bucket.

Larger items:

There are most likely other items in your garage that aren't mentioned here. While not every family will have all those mentioned, I have covered many items most commonly stored in the garage. Other items such as jet-skis, kayaks and boats, together with roof racks and trailers usually occupy another shed or area of garage separate from the cars, as do camper trailers and caravans.

Gardening equipment:

While equipment used in gardening and lawn care can be stored in the garage, it is more convenient to have a separate storage area if possible. Chemicals, mower fuel and oil that can be dangerous to children are safely stored away.

The Garden Shed:

Backyard garden sheds are a great way to store gardening tools in one place. Rakes and shovels stored in a garage can fall onto you or your car. The garden shed stores them out of the way while still being easily accessible. Most hardware stores offer shed kits, in a variety of sizes and prices, in wood, steel, or plastic and they can be installed in a weekend. Ensure you place the shed in an area that won't flood and consider placing it on a raised platform, useful in a temporary situation in a rental for instance, or on a concrete pad in a more permanent situation.

The magic of a tidy home also applies to the garden shed. Just as a tidy home equates to a tidy mind, the same principle applies with the garden shed.

It is often a lack of storage that makes for an untidy shed. For example, if you have the shed itself without any shelves, keeping everything tidy is going to be much more difficult.

Shelving:

A free-standing shelving unit available at hardware stores could be a solution that only requires assembly. It takes up a very small amount of floor space and comes in a number of shelf options. The top shelf is a safe place to store garden chemicals, such as weed killers, plant sprays, liquid and granulated fertilizers, and so on. Other shelves might house a plastic carry tote for seeds, planting tools and small items that you carry with you on planting day, twine, scissors, gloves, masks for use with potting mix, and any other smaller items that might otherwise get lost on the floor.

Care must be taken when storing corrosive chemicals on galvanised shelves. I have observed holes eaten through galvanised shelving and studs in a garden shed caused by leaking or spilt chemicals. Square plastic storage boxes or crates are ideal for storing chemicals on shelves. Plastic shelving is another option to consider.

Storage and maintenance:

Plastic bins or crates with lids are ideal for storing opened bags of potting mix and manure fertilizers for use over a period of time. Unopened bags can be stacked one on top of the other on the floor, or on a pallet to prevent moisture and maintain air circulation.

Ideally gardening tools should be stored in a cool, dry place. Moisture is the main cause of rust and rot on your tools and the sun and heat can cause handles to warp and crack. Ideal conditions are seldom found in many countries, making proper care of tools more important than ever. Before putting away any outdoor tools, clean them of all mud and dirt clumps that hold moisture, by rinsing them or using a wire brush to scrub and remove excess dirt. Remove sap from tools with turpentine and remove rust with vinegar. The life of wooden handles can be extended by regularly applying linseed oil. It prevents cracking and splintering and protects them from water and moisture. Linseed oil or a water displacement product can be applied to metal tools to protect them from rust. Coconut oil on a rag or paper towel is useful for wiping the blades of pruning shears.

Making use of available wall space to hang gardening tools is a more space efficient way to store them than storing them on the floor. Simply attach a piece of timber horizontally to the studs and screw on hooks at intervals to hang long handled tools such as rakes, forks, shovels and so on. Many gardening tools have a hole in the end of the handle. If there is no hole, it is a simple task to drill one.

The workbench provides useful space for potting up plants or repairing and sharpening tools. Wooden benches require staining to make them last and prevent the penetration of moisture. If space is unavailable in your shed, consider a plastic table with folding legs. Store it against the inside wall of your shed, simply take it outside to use for potting and hose it to clean it. Use it as an extra table when having a barbeque with friends by covering it with an attractive tablecloth.

Petrol lawn mowers need to be stored flat. Vertical storage can cause residual oil or fuel to seep into the engine and this can cause many issues. To save space, hang as many powered garden tools such as line trimmers, blowers, hedge trimmers, etc. as possible. However, prior to doing this ensure you check the manufacturer's recommendations for any reasons against storing them this way.

After discovering how you would like to store your tools and equipment, purchase the items necessary and move your equipment onto the lawn into categories. Place small hand tools such as trowels and spades into one area, larger tools such as rakes and shovels in another area. Dispose of or repair broken and damaged tools. Place motorised gear such as the motor mower, hedge trimmer and line trimmer together and clean and oil any neglected tools.

Now for the exciting part. Sweep out the shed, place your shelf unit where you planned, attach the timber to the studs and screw on the hooks ready to hang the large tools. Position one group at a time and stand back and admire a job well done. Remember, the more you can maintain tidiness in your shed, the less time you will spend searching for things, the more time you will have to sit and relax in your garden.

CONCLUSION

How many times have you heard, "there's no place like home," or "it's great to be home"? Home can be a castle or a tent or anything in between. Feelings of contentment, security and happiness don't depend on the type of home you live in, or 'things' you own, but more on reducing chaos in your world. Tidiness can turn 'ordinary' into 'magic'.

I am sure we have all experienced the feeling of satisfaction after a massive clean-up that was placed on the back burner because of overwhelm through not knowing where to start. There is also the experience of a sinking feeling when everything reverted to chaos when untidiness and clutter reappeared in a relatively short time.

Keep this book handy, refer to it often and remember how you felt when order was established. To restore order, the List of Contents page will guide you to the appropriate page without having to leaf through the whole book.

Remember to:
- return everything to its place after use.
- avoid hoarding because you 'just might need it further down the track', or 'this clothing item will fit me if I lose some weight'.
- dispose of or donate to charity the items that no longer serve you.

Enjoy:
- the feeling of being in control of your environment.
- a home full of joy where you experience sustenance, laugh with family members, have peaceful rest and feel safe and secure.
- a place where you can confidently invite friends to enjoy each other's company.
- setting an example for your children to follow so they too will know how to experience a life of order without chaos.
- the magic of a tidy home.

I look forward to hearing your comments about your experience of a tidy home. Please feel free to contact me at jeferguson33@gmail.com

BACK COVER

Tidiness in our homes and always being able to find what we are searching for results in less stress and anxiety in our lives. We all appreciate coming home to a tidy home. However, many of us don't know where to start or how to maintain tidiness once we have achieved it.

The Magic of a Tidy Home will enable you to discover:

- How mindset helps in achieving a tidy home
- How a tidy home can influence other areas of our lives
- How to get started now and avoid procrastination
- How to tidy each room, one at a time
- How to continuously maintain tidiness

Joy Ferguson has experienced a tidy home from her early childhood to today. She has written this book to share easy to follow tips to help you achieve the same the fast and easy way.

ISBN 978-0-646-81964-8

9 780646 819648 >

www.ingramcontent.com/pod-product-compliance
Lightning Source LLC
Chambersburg PA
CBHW071707040426
42446CB00011B/1960